Carole Chouinard and Randall Baer

Andrews and McMeel
A Universal Press Syndicate Company
Kansas City

Illustrations by Barrie Maguire

Library of Congress Cataloging-in-Publication Data

Chouinard, Carole.
    Making fun family videos / Carole Chouinard and Randall Baer.
        p.   cm.
    ISBN: 0-8362-2810-3 (pb) : $9.95
    1. Video tape recorders and recording—Amateurs' manuals.
    2. Video recordings—Production and direction—Amateurs'
    manuals. I. Baer, Randall. II. Title.
    TK9961.C485   1991
    791.45'023—dc20   91-12586
                                                              CIP

First Printing, April 1991
Second Printing, May 1991

Attention: Schools and Businesses

CONTENTS

PART III
SPECIAL OCCASIONS 89

ACKNOWLEDGMENTS

IT'S SAFE TO SAY that this book would never have been written had it not been for Victoria Houston's presence of mind to put a lunch conversation together with a glimmer of an idea for a book. She did just that, and here we have a book. She will probably be mildly relieved to know that we have never cursed her name—not even once—during the writing of this book. In fact, we are still excited about the whole book-writing process and are grateful that her creativity gave us this opportunity.

We could not have written this book without many people— friends, acquaintances, distant acquaintances, and strangers—who allowed us either to interview them or to view their own home videos. Through an extended network of friends and acquaintances we were able to contact people around the country and interview them about their home videotaping histories. The information we gathered was essential to this book and we deeply appreciate everyone who spoke with us or who sent us videos to watch.

We were also helped along by the encouragement of several friends who are writers by profession. We are grateful that they did not laugh hysterically when we announced our plans to write a book. We would like to thank our friends and coworkers who were generous with practical advice, moral support, and all sorts of information that made its way into the book.

Finally, we would like to offer our thanks and love to the two people who gave us a reason for making family videos in the first place—Annelise Andrea Baer and Darin Thomas Baer. For two preschoolers they exhibited patience above and beyond the call of duty. This book is dedicated to Annelise and Darin in hopes that we will be able to give them a video legacy of the joy and love they have brought to us.

INTRODUCTION

O YOU HAVE FUN when you use your camcorder? We mean really have fun? The same kind of fun kids have when they're goofing around in front of an audience? The kind of fun that comes from catching a loved one in a slightly embarrassing moment? The kind of fun that makes for great family videos that everyone loves to watch? You don't?

People hide when you bring out your camcorder? Your kids don't want to have birthday parties anymore? Even your closest family members won't sit through an evening of your best videos? Well, if this sounds more like your life, you have a problem. You have a bad case of boring home videos.

As part of the in-depth research for this book we took it upon ourselves to view countless hours of home videos and as a result, we've come to one conclusion. The plain truth is, no matter how dull you feel your videos are, you are not alone. You can bet that for every ten seconds of hilarity on "America's Funniest Home Videos," any one of those participating families has hours of the same old dull family videos that you have on your shelf. It may seem ironic but the world is full of people shooting hours of home videos that nobody wants to watch. And yes, each of us has the potential to turn an innocent camcorder into an electronic party killer.

So what are we doing wrong? We are living with one of the marvels of the ages and hardly anyone is having fun using it. Where's all the enjoyment? Where's the excitement? Where's that sense of intimacy that should be captured whenever we bring out our camcorder? Why is it that so few of us can make a watchable fun home video?

Let's take a few minutes here to reflect on the camcorder phenomenon. Most of us are of a generation where home movies were a fact of life. If your family didn't have an 8mm camera, then one of your neighbors or relatives surely did. Very few of us ever managed to avoid the helpless feeling that came from knowing we would have to spend a long, dull, soundless evening watching someone's home movies. We've seen them all—birthday movies, Christmas movies, and, worst of all, vacation movies. Hours of movies, years of movies, all spliced together into one two-hour chunk of home movie purgatory. We'll try not to remind you of the scintillating narration that accompanied them either.

Added to this legacy is the fact that we've all come of age with television. After twenty-five or thirty years of watching TV most of us can unconsciously recognize all of the different television formats. It's a fair bet that you could put this book down and easily describe the basic formula for any TV sitcom, news program, game show, or TV movie. We're also handicapped by the fact that we bring to our home videos the lofty standards of a professionally produced television show. When most of us pick up a camcorder we somehow assume that our camera movements will flow effortlessly. There will be smooth zooms in on the birthday boy or girl, our pans to the left or right will glide gracefully and at just the right speed. And, of course, our finished video will make perfect sense from beginning to end. Any viewer who's lucky enough to see the finished product will be instantly captivated.

But if even your eyes glaze over at the thought of watching your own home videos, you should pause a few minutes to think about what you're putting on tape and how you're actually making those videos. A few basic technical tips might be all it takes to help you be more creative behind the camera. Maybe just thinking about shooting in a more organized manner will help too. Either way, taking some time to think about how you should record an event will definitely make for more enjoyable home videos.

Now, please don't get the feeling that just because we're writing this book we're any different from you. We've made many of the same mistakes in our own videos that you've made in yours. We've shot dull videos, out-of-focus videos, dark videos, and videos with blue people. We've got some great videos that are priceless and some videos that only a parent would love. What we have done over the course of years is make the camcorder a normal feature of our household. We've sort of demystified the whole taping process—we don't just save it for extraspecial occasions where its appearance triggers stagy responses and unnatural actions. Our camcorder is always easily accessible so we can grab it and record those precious slice-of-life moments that always pop up.

We've also developed some creative ideas that have truly broadened the scope of our home videos. These ideas have made it fun for us to use our camcorder. In fact, using our camcorder often enhances our activities instead of merely letting us record them.

Which leads us to a major point we will return to throughout this book. We feel that everyone should strike a balance between documenting an event and participating in it. We're firm believers that every second of every special event does not need to be committed to videotape. There comes a time when you need to put down the camera and experience the event with your family. We also believe that you don't need to take the camcorder along to every event. We've found that when we do take the camera, we have a great time at the event and making the videotape. When we don't take the camcorder along we still have a great family event.

A second point we'll keep stressing is that all of your family members who are physically able should know how to use your camcorder. Remember those old home movies? Where was dad during those vacations? Where was he at the birthday parties or at the family reunion? Dad was behind the camera because, in those tradition-conscious times, dad was the only person who knew how to run the camera. Today when you watch those old home movies you miss not seeing dad, don't you? That's our point. Good family videos should include the whole family, not everybody minus one.

Finally, the most important message we'll try to get across is that you must make time for your family to be together—be it merely to play or to have some special event. What's important is to encourage the one-on-one interaction between children, parents, grandparents, and friends. The inevitable mistakes that come from trying to juggle participating and documenting will be a part of the entire look of your home video. Jerky zoom shots and abrupt cuts will not diminish how your family values the documentation of their days.

Essentially, our thought is this: Take time to learn a few technical tricks, begin to incorporate some creativity into your videos, **have fun** while you're taping, and, most important, create those family activities that will transform your videos into cherished memories.

Part I
GETTING TO KNOW YOUR CAMCORDER
(This Is Fun?)

HEN YOU GET DOWN TO IT, there are only two essential requirements for making fun family videos—a family and a camcorder. We're proceeding on the assumptions that you already have some semblance of a family and that you probably have some video equipment, or that you're close to making your purchase.

To help you share in all this "fun" we talk about, we will give you a quick tour of the camcorder features and take you through some common mistakes that people make with their equipment. Then we'll teach you a technique to make your home videos move faster and simply enthrall all viewers.

Once you triumph over the common mistakes and have a few professional tricks up your sleeve, you'll find yourself thinking, Hey, this video actually looks good. It's enjoyable to watch. This is fun!

1
BUYING A CAMCORDER
(The Fun Begins)

F YOU ARE one of the dwindling minority who haven't yet bought a camcorder, it's time to get out there and do it. Over three million were sold in 1990. Every day you keep putting it off will be one more day you'll miss out on capturing once-in-a-lifetime family events. Nobody ever regrets buying a camcorder so if your reason for putting it off is that all the technical jargon sounds like a foreign language to you, wait no more. We will guide you along by helping you sort out the gobbledygook and showing you what you need in a camcorder and what you can live without.

In camcorders as in life, it really does pay to look before you buy. But with 150 different models available, how do you determine which ones are for you and which aren't? The answer we have come up with is fairly simple. Ask yourself these four basic questions—

1. What would you like to record with your camcorder?
★ Tape your children's development and family activities?
★ Tape vacations or other travels?
★ Tape sporting events and practice sessions?

2. How much money can you afford to spend?

If the sky's the limit, you'll be a welcome customer in any electronics store. For $1,800–$2,500 you can buy a top-of-the-line camcorder in any of the various formats available. If you're like most of us and still want something that's good but won't be obsolete in three years, $1,100–$1,800 will get you out the door with a very nice piece of equipment. But if you still want a camcorder and your price range is slightly more modest, $600–$1,100 will let you join in the fun without worrying about owning an electronic Edsel. If anything under $600 catches your eye, watch out. You are probably being asked to give up some crucial features or, even worse, to buy outdated technology.

3. How proficient are you with any kind of electronic equipment?

The worst thing that can happen to you is to walk out of the store with a $1,500 camcorder that you're afraid to touch. It is important to stay with cameras that are at your own proficiency level. If you end up buying a piece of complicated equipment that you can't figure out how to use, how can you make any fun family videos? Our advice: only buy a camcorder that you feel comfortable using.

4. How "good" do you want your videos to look?

The distinction between "home" and "professional" features is an area that the camcorder manufacturers are blurring more and more each year. This year's top-of-the-line features will most likely become bottom-of-the-line standards in only a few years. Automatic focus and digital effects like titling were available only on the most expensive models not so long ago. Now even the least expensive camcorders offer these features and more. In fact, the picture quality on some home camcorders can surpass most of what you watch on your TV set every day. So, beware. The extra money you end up spending on some camcorders may be for bells and whistles and not necessarily for improved picture quality.

FORMATS

Now that you've given some thought to what you'd like to record, how much money to spend, and how good you'd like your videos to look, it's time to start making some decisions. The first area up is: format.

Camcorders are available in seven different formats. The term *format* refers to the type of tape cassette each camcorder uses and only partially to the camcorder's cost or picture quality. If you already own some sort of home video system (VCR, stereo, television, and the like), it can have a big influence on your buying decision. The reason: most camcorder formats are *not* compatible with each other. By "compatible" we mean that you can remove a videocassette from your camcorder, drop it straight into your home VCR, and press PLAY. Unless you intend to overhaul your current home system, you will probably want to stay within the same format. For example, if you already own one or two VHS videocassette recorders and have a small closet full of cassettes, you may lean toward buying a camcorder that's VHS compatible.

However, the manufacturers have introduced a little twist that makes your life easier while making your decision a little more complicated. If a camcorder format is not compatible with your home system, that doesn't mean you still can't play back a camcorder tape anywhere, anytime. All camcorders give you the option of simply running a short video cable from your camcorder into any TV set or VCR. Then, all you need do is play back your recorded tape right from the camcorder itself.

Even though you may choose to stay with the convenience of being able to drop a camcorder tape directly into your VCR, you need not keep all your equipment in the same format. Our personal video equipment is in both the VHS and the 8mm formats, and we find it quite simple merely to plug the camcorder in whenever we want to watch tapes. It's just another decision you have to make and feel comfortable with.

Let's look at each of these seven formats in a little more detail.

Full-Size VHS

This is the format with which most of us are familiar—the standard seven-by-four-inch cassette that offers perfectly acceptable video quality for the average home VCR. It has been around for ages and is by far the most popular format around.

Good news: If you buy a Full-Size VHS camcorder, all you have to do is tape whatever you like, then drop the cassette into your home VCR and press PLAY.

Bad news: A VHS camcorder isn't quite on the cutting edge of picture quality anymore. Its basic technology dates from 1970 and just about every bit of performance has been squeezed out of it.

VHS Compact (VHS-C)

VHS-C was introduced as a way of making VHS camcorders smaller and lighter. It uses videocassettes that are about one-third the size of a full-size VHS tape, which allows the rest of the camcorder to be much smaller too. To make this smaller cassette compatible with a Full-Size VHS VCR, a special adaptor shell must be used. The VHS-C cassette is first placed inside the adaptor shell, then the entire assembly is loaded into a "standard" VHS machine.

Good news: You maintain compatibility with the VHS format and get a much smaller, lighter camcorder.

Bad news: You need to go through the routine of using an adaptor shell whenever you play back the tapes on a standard VHS machine. And because of the smaller cassette size, you are limited to thirty minutes of recording time in normal, Standard-Play speed.

Super VHS (S-VHS)

This is one of the two formats that bring home camcorders into the realm of professional-broadcast quality. The state-of-the-art technology it uses creates a picture that has nearly twice the detail and sharpness of a standard VHS picture.

Good news: Great picture quality.

Bad news: Two things are required to make all this quality available—a newer model, high-resolution television set and special videocassettes. You can watch S-VHS tapes on a regular television set or even record on regular VHS cassettes, but neither will give you the high-quality picture you have paid for. Another drawback is that the S-VHS format is not compatible with the standard VHS format. S-VHS tapes cannot be played back in a standard VHS VCR, so you either need an S-VHS VCR or need to play back all of the tapes from the camcorder itself. On the plus side, though, you can play back standard VHS tapes on an S-VHS VCR or camcorder. However you look at it, if you want to play the video game at this level, expect to pay for the quality you're getting.

S-VHS Compact

Essentially, this format works on the same principle as the VHS-C format we talked about earlier. All the S-VHS technology has merely been downsized to allow a smaller, lighter camcorder.

Good news: S-VHS quality in a small package.
Bad news: The same problems of having to use an adaptor shell and being limited to thirty minutes of recording time per cassette.

8mm

The 8mm format is exploding in popularity. It uses videocassettes that are the size of an audiocassette, yet delivers up to two hours of recording time. The 8mm camcorders are pushing the size limits by becoming truly "hand held" and are setting the size standard that VHS-C is struggling to match.

Good news: Models are available in styles ranging from shoulder size to palm size. You get two hours of taping time and picture quality that is comparable to full-size VHS.
Bad news: The 8mm format is incompatible with all VHS formats, requiring you either to buy an 8mm VCR for your home or to live with connecting the camcorder up to your TV set every time you wish to play back a tape.

High Band 8mm (or Hi8)

In the constant game of catchup that the camcorder manufacturers play, Hi8 is the return salvo that 8mm has fired at the Super VHS format. It, too, offers a major improvement in picture quality over standard 8mm and very nearly matches the quality of S-VHS.

Good news: Superior picture quality along with the size benefits of the 8mm format.

Bad news: Like S-VHS, this format must have a television set that will accommodate the improved picture quality it delivers. Moreover, Hi8 tapes are *not* compatible with standard 8mm VCRs, but 8mm tapes are playable on a Hi8 camcorder or VCR.

Extended Definition Beta (ED Beta)

Poor old Beta! It was the very first home video format to be introduced and now it's nearly nonexistent. The other formats have become so popular that it is now almost impossible to find Beta equipment or videocassettes. The people who own Beta tend to swear by it, touting better colors and image quality than either VHS or 8mm. Although Beta is still quite a big seller on the international market, SONY Corporation (the only manufacturer of Beta) has thrown in the towel in the United States. Extended Definition (ED) Beta is the only Beta format still being offered in this country. The quality of this format is quite stunning, though. Its resolution (sharpness) is better than either S-VHS or Hi8 and its colors are crisper and richer. An ED Beta camcorder is top of the line as far as home camcorders go and is actually comparable to some of the broadcast-quality cameras the professionals use.

Good news: Great picture quality, fully professional features, and the camaraderie of other Beta-philes (when you can find them).
Bad news: Cost, incompatibility with any other format, difficulty in buying support equipment.

T I P

Our advice is to make camcorder size a deciding factor in your purchase. The majority of people we spoke with felt that heavy, bulky equipment kept them from taking their camcorders more places. Smaller camcorders make it much easier for you to grab your camera and go.

FEATURES

Now that we've introduced you to the different formats, it's time to start thinking about features. You will need to make a couple of decisions here because not all features are standard on all camcorders. Most are treated as options and you need to decide whether they are worth the extra money.

Auto Focus

· Auto Focus is now a standard item on nearly all camcorders and is definitely worth the money. *Auto*matic focus means just that: the camcorder automatically focuses itself no matter where you aim it. As a result, you are now free to concentrate on creating videos and not on having to keep things in focus. Auto Focus systems aren't always foolproof, but for the novice camera operator they're a great feature to have and nearly worth their weight in gold.

Manual Override Controls

These controls are essential features to have with any automatic camcorder system. Modern electronics can make the new generation of camcorders do some pretty eye-opening things, but occasions will arise when you will want to take control over things yourself. Any camcorder you consider buying should offer you the option of manually setting focus, iris setting, and color balance.

Manual Focus Override. Auto Focus systems are often fooled under certain conditions. The best example of this is when you try shooting a subject that is on the other side of a piece of glass, like a door or window. Often the Auto Focus system will try to focus on the glass itself and not on the object you're interested in. The resulting confusion can give you either an out-of-focus picture or one that bounces in and out of focus as the camera tries to figure things out. The manual override feature allows you to take control and focus the lens on the image you feel is important.

Iris Setting. The iris on a camcorder performs the same function as the iris in your eye—it controls the amount of light entering and automatically adjusts for bright or dark conditions. The camcorder's iris either opens or closes according to decisions made by its electronics, which can often be fooled. If your subject is either darker or lighter than its background, a camcorder will often adjust itself for the background and not your subject. As a result, you may end up with a dark silhouette instead of a nicely exposed picture. Most camcorders have a BACKLIGHT button, which compensates to some extent. But in situations like this, it is always better to take control yourself and rely on your own eye.

Color Correction or White Balance. All camcorders need some sort of reference to tell them what color your subject should be. Most models now adjust the color automatically, depending on whether you are shooting under incandescent lights, fluorescent lights, in the shade, or in bright sunlight. If a camcorder doesn't adjust correctly, you can end up with blue or orange flesh tones, neither of which is very flattering. Times will arise when it will be nice to have a say in what color things should be. With the ability to manually set white balance, you can actually alter the colors so people appear warmer or even make old-fashioned sepia-toned videos. If you plan to get more involved in your taping or even go for an occasional arty effect, this control is an important asset.

Light Levels

One of the greatest features that today's camcorders have is the ability to make good-quality pictures under very low lighting conditions. If your primary reason for buying a camcorder is to tape your children and family, many of your photo opportunities will come indoors, under normal, home lighting conditions. To help you decide, all camcorders are rated as to how many lux they require to make a good picture. Lux is simply an international reference standard for measuring the amount of light striking an object. Basically, the darker a room is the lower the lux level. A camcorder that makes good pictures in normal, indoor situations will have a lux rating in the eight to fifteen range. All you really need to remember, though, is—the lower a camcorder's lux rating the better it is at making low-light-level pictures.

Variable High-Speed Shutter

Another benefit of solid-state electronics has been the introduction of the variable high-speed shutter. Normally, a camcorder operates with an effective shutter speed of only 1/30th of a second. Compared to the 35mm still cameras most of us own, this is really quite slow. It's only because a camcorder's video images are changing at thirty frames per second that we can get away with it at all. With the introduction of slow-motion/freeze-frame VCRs, people started complaining that some of their slow-motion playbacks were blurry and fuzzy. The reason is, if you look at a video playback one frame at a time, 1/30th of a second is just too slow of a shutter speed to give a sharp, slow-motion replay of your child's baseball swing.

Having a variable-speed shutter allows you to eliminate this problem. Now you have the option of increasing the effective shutter speed all the way up to 1/10,000th of a second with some camcorders. Suddenly, a whole range of crisp, high-speed video opportunities are now open to us.

To take advantage of this feature, though, there must be plenty of light available. Each time you increase the shutter speed (say, from 1/100th to 1/250th) you cut down on the amount of light reaching the camcorder's electronics. However, with this newfound ability to increase shutter speeds, you can now experiment with a whole range of slow-motion and stop-actions events.

Flying Erase Head

No, this isn't the name of some new fringe rock group. This is, in fact, a feature that should be standard on all camcorders. A flying erase head is an extra mechanism inside the camcorder that allows it to make a clean edit every time you start and stop recording. The individual shots can now butt seamlessly together without any "breakup" or "hash" between them. This is one of those important features that will instantly make all of your videos look better.

Sound Systems

A good-quality sound system is something that most people don't really think about—that is, until they realize that the system they're listening to isn't. Camcorders have the technical capability to reproduce sound at nearly the same quality level as a compact disc. Some camcorders are even available with high-fidelity stereo sound. This may sound like a great idea, but you won't be able to appreciate any of this superb sound quality unless you already own a stereo system through which to play it back. Maybe you can live without having true stereo, but high-fidelity sound should be a must on any camcorder, along with the option of being able to change microphones. You may never need or want to use a different microphone on your camera, but it's a simple enough feature and you will appreciate it if the occasion should arise.

Lenses

Zoom lenses are now standard features on all camcorders. By pressing a button or moving a lever you can adjust from a wide shot to closeup or vice versa. Once you master the artful technique of the smooth zoom, you're well on your way to creative videotaping. Rest assured, though, that perfecting this skill will drive you and your viewers a little batty. Only practice and time will keep your videos from bouncing up and down, forward and backward at a roller-coaster pace.

Most camcorders even come with a Macro Focus capability, which allows you to focus on an object so close it's physically touching the lens. Extreme closeups of flowers, insects, household items, even children's faces are now within your reach at the mere push of a button.

We hope that some of the camcorder jargon we've gone over is now a little clearer to you than it was before we started. Many features and options are available with all camcorders and we've given only the once-over to some of the most important. We should warn you that you will still need to know something about title and effects generators, auxiliary lights, tripods, and numerous other accessories. If you are seriously shopping for a new camcorder, go to your local newsstand or library. There are several magazines and books available specifically designed to help you get through the decision-making process.

Salespeople at reputable dealerships can usually be counted on as being somewhat knowledgeable about the different features offered, although you know as well as we do that salespeople are looking for a sale. You are the only person who knows why you want a camcorder, so the better prepared you are the easier the entire shopping process will be. If you do your homework by reading up and asking friends about their camcorders, you will have a pretty good idea of what you're looking for before you ever walk into a camcorder store.

2
COMMON TECHNICAL MISTAKES

(The Frustration Begins)

T IS OUR HOPE that after you read this chapter your videos will look 100 percent better. This is because, in our research, we noticed that nearly everyone makes the same technical mistakes with the camcorder. It's all understandable since not many owners of camcorders earn their living by shooting videos. Since one of us does just that, it was quite obvious to see that a few simple mistakes were being repeated over and over again. After you finish reading this chapter, choose one of your tapes at random and pop it into your VCR. See how many of these simple mistakes you have made. Then, just before you use your camcorder again, pick up this book and glance over 'ol chapter 2 once again. The best way to learn is from your own mistakes. Then make a concerted effort not to repeat those mistakes.

MISTAKE 1
PANNING YOUR CAMCORDER TOO QUICKLY

Result: Shots that are blurred, jerky, and uncomfortable to watch.
Solution: Slow down your camera moves.

Picture this scenario: You've taken your brand new camcorder out to the backyard and you're looking to record some videos of your children playing. While you're in the middle of shooting a great close-up of your son's muddy face an off-camera voice suddenly calls out, "Hey, everybody look at what I found!" Instinctively, you whip your camcorder around to show us who yelled out. In a matter of mere seconds you manage to zoom in, focus up, and show us the result—your neighbor's kid gingerly holding a giant snail.

If this sounds as if it could be one of your shots—blame your instincts. They've let you down again. Only when you play this shot back do you realize that all you've managed to record is a muddy kid close up, a blur of color, concluded by a jerky shot of a kid with a snail. The professionals actually have a name for this type of camera move; it's called a "whip pan," and you've just executed a doozy.

There's one quick and easy solution for this common problem—*slow down your camera moves.*

Whenever you're using your camcorder it's nearly impossible to make a camera move that is too slow. Zooms, tilts, and pans should always be as smooth and as slow as you can make them. Even if you feel that you're making your moves much too slowly, you're probably not.

There's actually a good reason for this. When viewers are watching your tapes their eyes are continuously scanning the picture to see all the points of interest. First, they'll look at one point, and another, and then another, until they've looked at everything that seems to be interesting. By the time they're bored with all of the elements in one shot it's up to you to give them something new and interesting to look at.

It's precisely because your viewers' eyes are constantly scanning the picture that you can get away with slow camera moves. Even during those occasions when their ears hear something that their eyes don't see, they'll keep scanning the picture looking for what it is they are hearing. When you whip pan your camcorder from one shot to the next, your viewers' eyes get disoriented because you've left them nothing interesting to focus on. But, if you take four or five seconds to complete your pan, their eyes will always have something to look at while their ears keep busy listening to the sound.

It's crucial to remember that you and your camcorder provide the *entire* point of reference for those watching your videotapes. Your audience "see" nothing until you decide to show it to them. Your job is always to show them things as smoothly and as naturally as possible. And what's the key to being smooth and natural? *Slow down those camera moves.*

MISTAKE 2
RECORDING INDIVIDUAL SHOTS
THAT ARE TOO LONG

Result: Five- to ten-minute chunks of tape that are boring.
Solution: Limit your shots to a more viewable length.

Scenario two: You're still shooting a video of your kids playing in the yard. The recently discovered snail is now crawling across a leaf to a chorus of "yuks" and "grosses." In a flash of creativity, you decide on a much closer shot of the snail. You take a couple of steps forward (camcorder running, of course), try to frame up, and discover that you're still not quite close enough. So, you walk a little closer, frame up, zoom in, and now discover that you're completely out of focus. By the time you do get the camera focused and manage to find the snail, you've used up thirty or forty seconds of videotape and produced a completely unwatchable piece of video. In fact, to an impartial viewer (the best kind) it looks as if you were trying to record all of this while one of the kids was clutching your leg. And by the way, you weren't wearing a blindfold, were you?

This kind of camera shot is easy to analyze because it manages to include four of our six most common mistakes. Besides the whip pan, there are: walking around with the camera running, too much zooming, and the unforgivable out-of-focus shot.

When you get down to it, though, the main problem here is simply not knowing when to stop recording. Even if everything in our scenario had been done smoothly and slowly, it would still serve us well to know when to stop recording. We have a quick and easy rule of thumb to help you avoid this mistake—*keep most of your shots between seven and ten seconds long.*

You can begin to teach yourself this solution by silently counting to ten each time you start recording. When you reach ten, stop the tape and look for a new shot. Of course, occasionally you will want to record something for longer than ten seconds. When you do, be certain the action warrants the extra length—a person talking about something specific or concluding a definite action. But, for the average shot the average length should be seven to ten seconds. A shot can always be longer or shorter, but if it's longer, you should be the one who makes the conscious decision to keep recording.

Once you start to get the hang of shooting ten-second pieces of video you'll be ready to learn more about the framework for editing as you shoot. In Chapter 3 we will discuss this process in detail, but for now memorize rule 2—*If there is no specific action or dialogue taking place, limit your shots to ten seconds.*

MISTAKE 3
ACCIDENTLY LEAVING YOUR
CAMCORDER RUNNING

Result: Surreal videos that nobody else wants to watch.
Solution: Remember to check that your camcorder has stopped recording.

May we mention that you have only to suffer through watching the end result of this mistake just once to know what we mean? You've seen it before. The tape comes on. We see . . . gray, lots of gray. It looks . . . kind of stony, like cement, and . . . it's moving. What is it? How can it move? We watch, more quizzical than enthralled. It's . . . a sidewalk! But why are we watching it? We hear voices but they don't seem to know that we're here, watching and listening. Maybe the voices will tell us why we're watching a sidewalk? Tell us, voices! As we keep watching we can make out that someone is carrying the camcorder—it must be slung over a shoulder on a strap—and walking. Someone has left the camcorder recording, so we must be watching either a mistake or a performance art piece. Is it a mistake? Is it art? It's a mistake.

There's only one way to prevent this mistake—*always check to see that your camcorder has stopped recording whenever you're finished.*

Not only will this helpful tip save you from the embarrassment of a sidewalk-to-nowhere incident; it will also save you from running out of tape and batteries if you happen to set your camcorder down and leave it running. Remind yourself always to glance at the record/talley light in the viewfinder or at the one on the front of the camera every time you stop recording. Or, glance at the tape counter readout window or at the videocassette itself. If the record/talley light is still on, or if the tape counter numbers are counting, or if the tape spools are still moving, you've forgotten to stop recording. As soon as you develop the habit of taking a look at any one of these, you'll find that you are catching yourself much more often than you would have ever thought.

T I P

Our prize for the "best example of accidentally leaving your camcorder running" goes to the video we saw of floor, tinny-sounding chatter, the sound of a door closing, then feet—several pairs of feet—a whoosh of water, more doors closing, and finally some water running. You guessed it. Some unknowing soul actually recorded a trip to the restroom.

Learn from the mistakes of others. Always check to see that your camcorder has stopped recording. After all, it's possible that your mistake could be even more embarrassing than this one.

Of course, if your problem is just the opposite—thinking you're recording when you're not—there isn't much we can do to help. Except point out that the little red light in the viewfinder is there for a reason. It's up to you, the camcorder artist, to figure out why it isn't lighted when you think you're taping.

MISTAKE 4
SHOOTING TEN-MINUTE VIDEOS FROM ONLY ONE SPOT (CEMENT SHOES SYNDROME)

Result: Dull videos—too much zooming and not enough closeups.
Solution: Move around—get closer to your subject.

Picture, if you will, a videotape so incredibly dull that it looks as if a statue-come-to-life had been using your camcorder. Children are playing . . . way over there. People are watching those children . . . way over here. The point of reference for you, the viewer, is neither here nor there. You're stuck forever in the middle—stuck in the twilight zone of camcordery. Forever doomed to watching home videos shot by someone who forgot that he could move.

Sound familiar? Seen one or two videos that might fit this category? Well, rest easy. We can guarantee that this malady will never affect your home videos. All you need to do is follow our example and learn the simple trick of moving your feet.

Too many home videos are static and dull because they never achieve any intimacy with their subject. The people who shoot them too often seem struck by the same mysterious malady time and time again. For some reason, as soon as tape starts rolling they pick one spot and plant themselves there until they're done taping. They never move, never get closer to their subjects, never look for better angles. The only movement we see comes from zooming in and out, in and out, in and out. The resulting videos are dull because they don't convey a crucial element—a feeling of intimacy. Their poor viewers never even come close to getting a feel for what it was like to be there.

The solution for this mistake: move around. Pick shorter-length shots and learn to change positions every time you stop tape. Always keep looking for better, more flattering angles of your subject. Once you start getting closer to people you'll find that a sense of intimacy begins to develop all by itself. Remember, you and your camcorder are your viewers' only point of reference. When you begin to vary your shots selectively and start moving around, you'll be creating visual interest for your viewers. And when you begin to create visual interest, you'll find that you're venturing into that area of control the world refers to as creativity. All it takes is a combination of varying shots, an ordered pattern and, voilà, you're well on your way to learning editing as you shoot (Chapter 3). Funny how it all seems to tie together, isn't it?

MISTAKE 5
SHOOTING VIDEOS WHEN THERE'S NOT ENOUGH LIGHT

Result: "Nightscope" videos that don't look quite as you remember them.

Solution: Use an auxiliary light to enhance the natural look.

Your camcorder can perform some dazzling tricks. One of its best is the ability to record videos under extremely low lighting conditions. In fact, one of the major selling points for new camcorders is this very ability to make a decent picture with very little light. Some models can record in as little as 1 lux of light, and 1 lux, friends, is barely enough light to read in, let alone make a very good video picture.

When you try to record under these very low-light levels, your camcorder electronically enhances the picture so that the image will appear bright enough. Sometimes this little trick will make your low-light videos look as if they were shot with a military night scope. The better cameras just make your videos look unnaturally bright, but the lesser ones can make them appear noisy, with little flecks of white static throughout the picture.

The way to beat this problem, and make your indoor videos look 100 percent better, is to use an auxiliary light. Most of the newer lights on the market are designed specifically to give your camcorder picture that little extra oomph it needs. At sizes ranging from ten to fifty watts, they are small and light enough to be mounted directly on your camera. Because they aren't overly bright, your subjects will appear much more natural than they would if you were using an older-style 150-watt spotlight and beaming it directly into their eyes.

A second added benefit to the newer lights is that many of them operate on rechargeable batteries. You can get anywhere from twenty minutes to a half hour of use from each charge. This is an ideal length for 99 percent of what you would ever shoot indoors. If for some reason you need an extra light for a longer time, you also have the option of using a 120-volt adaptor and running the light from a standard wall outlet. In fact, these lights have become such a hot idea that a couple of manufacturers are now offering them already built into some of their higher end camcorders. Auxiliary lights are rapidly becoming the video equivalent of a still camera's built-in electronic flash. You may not use them all the time, but they'll surely come in handy once in a while.

With just the couple of extra lux you get from one of these auxiliary lights you'll notice a big improvement in the look of your indoor videos. The colors will be brighter and more natural, and people's faces will look much more attractive. If you haven't seen one of these lights in use yet, you'll just have to trust us on this one. If you plan to use your camcorder to shoot indoor videos (birthday parties, the kids taking baths, playing, etc.), one of these auxiliary lights will be well worth the extra investment.

MISTAKE 6
SHOOTING SUBJECTS WITH A
BRIGHT BACKGROUND BEHIND THEM

Result: Dark, silhouetted people with overly bright backgrounds.
Solution: Place subjects so light isn't directly behind them.

Here's a top contender for producing some of the most unwatchable videos of all time. If you haven't run up against this yet, just wait. Sooner or later everyone gets caught and you'll be lucky if you get caught only once or twice. Even the camcorder manufacturers recognize that strong backlighting is a major problem. If it weren't, why are they working so hard to come up with a foolproof solution?

The typical backlighted scenario is deceptively simple: A couple of people merely standing in front of a bright window. That's it, no big deal. Everything looks okay to your eye, but when you frame up your camcorder all you get is a nicely exposed window with a couple of dark shadows standing in front of it. You can help this somewhat by turning on the camcorder's "backlight" switch, but the video picture you end up with will never really look as good as it does to your eye.

All a camcorder's backlight switch does is tell the electronic circuits that you're interested in the foreground subjects and not the bright window behind them. Using this switch can help considerably, but it's best to remember that it's nowhere near being foolproof. When the backlight circuit does work well, you'll end up with foreground subjects being adjusted well enough to see. When it doesn't work so well, you'll end up with silhouettes. Actually, current camcorder technology doesn't yet offer us a decent way to split the difference, so until something new is developed it is best to avoid this problem entirely by following a couple of tips.

The best solution to a bad backlighting situation is to avoid it whenever possible. If you've got the time, change positions (either yours or that of your subjects). It's always preferable to have the light shining directly on your subjects' faces, not on their backs. If possible, move them. If that isn't an option, you should try moving to one side or the other. Look for a camera position where the bright background isn't directly behind your subject. If you have to, consider sacrificing the look of your shot. It's better to be off to one side of a person than to have a distractingly "hot" background behind them.

If neither you nor your subject can move, and you've just got to have this shot, try to exclude as much of the bright background as possible. Zoom in as tightly as you can but still keep a comfortable shot. A well exposed closeup shot of two talking heads is better than a waist-sized medium shot of two people with a white-hot background. Be sure to use your camcorder's backlight switch too. The electronics may not be foolproof but they will surely help make this kind of shot look considerably better than it would without them.

THE "I COULD KILL MYSELF" CAMCORDER MISTAKES

Remember, we're here to help. Occasionally you'll make a mistake that's so, well, stupid that you'll wonder if you shouldn't just put that old camcorder away forever. Even in your darkest moments of despair, don't let yourself think that you're the only person who's ever made such a dumb mistake. We've all been caught before—maybe we're too proud now to admit it, but we've all spent time with our head in our hands moaning, Why? How? We'll bet that even the boldest camera operator among you will find himself or herself somewhere in this next section.

"I COULD KILL MYSELF" MISTAKE 1
HAVING YOUR BATTERIES GO DEAD

Your camcorder is really nothing short of a miraculous invention. It's always ready, just waiting for you to pick it up and capture life at a moment's notice. There's only one teensy, weensy problem—camcorders don't run by themselves; they run on batteries.

For anyone who has ever used a camcorder, batteries have got to be the number one frustration of all time. Rechargeable Ni-Cad batteries are great, but they always seem to have the nasty habit of being run down when you need them the most. It's a sad fact of life that even though you can recharge Ni-Cads several hundred times, once they are fully charged they begin the slow process of losing that charge, all by themselves. A fully charged Ni-Cad can lose nearly 20 percent of its power the first week and all it has to do is just sit there inside your camcorder. If it sits longer, say two or three weeks, it's a certain bet that the low battery light will begin flashing just seconds after you turn your camcorder on.

Since there is no easy way to tell how much charge is left in each battery, your best solution is to try to keep them all fully charged at all times. This may sound as if it will be a hassle, but give it a try anyway. Set up your battery charger in an out-of-the-way place and keep your batteries in it until you're ready to use them. When you feel like recording something, grab your camcorder, pop in a battery, and go. This way your batteries will always be fully charged and you'll be guaranteed to get as much out of them as they've got to give.

On those occasions when you'll be shooting all day, and especially if you're traveling, always carry one or two spare batteries with you. Be sure they're fully charged, then just drop them into your bag or pocket. Never try to get along with just one battery. You'll always regret it. Have at least two batteries with you at all times, and if you can afford it buy a third. Extra batteries are small, easy to carry, and worth their weight in gold. You'll thank us for this advice when your afternoon's shooting is saved because you had a spare.

T I P

If you own more than one battery, take a few seconds to mark each with an identifying letter. Use an indelible marker and label one *A*, one *B*, one *C*, etc. This will make it much easier to keep track of each battery as you use it. If you use only batteries A and B today, be sure to recharge them first. When they're recharged, pop battery C in for a little top-off. Tomorrow, start off with battery C, then move on to A and B. Keep rotating your batteries like this for as long as you use them. If any one of them starts to act up, you'll be able to single it out much faster than you would if they all looked the same.

And while we're on spare batteries, let's talk about comfort. Not your comfort—the batteries' comfort. If it's very cold or extremely hot, they will hold less of a charge than they would at a nice seventy-two degrees.

When it's cold, keep them inside your coat where your body heat will keep them warm. If you leave them in a carrying bag or an outside coat pocket, they'll soon reach the same temperature as the outside air. When batteries get too cold they can lose up to half of their charge before you've even started shooting. Batteries that are too hot will behave similarly. If it's hot outside, keep them as cool as possible. Both heat and cold will sap the life from a freshly charged battery and that can leave you high and dry when you're in the middle of a day's shooting. If you will be shooting in either extreme, keep your batteries comfortable.

"I COULD KILL MYSELF" MISTAKE 2
RUNNING OUT OF TAPE

The partner to having dead batteries is running out of tape. Fortunately, this doesn't happen quite as often as running out of battery power. When you run out of tape, though, your day's shooting is over. Both spare tapes and extra batteries are light and small enough that there isn't any excuse for not carrying them with you. This is especially true if your camcorder is in either the VHS-C or the 8mm format. Make a habit of slipping some extras into your pocket or bag and you won't even notice that they're there.

In a related matter, have you ever accidently left your camcorder running when you thought it was turned off? The first time this happens to you, and it will, be cool. The day isn't ruined. All you need do is rewind your videotape to the last piece of "good" video and start reshooting from there. The reason videotape was invented in the first place was so that people could reuse it. You would be considered almost unpatriotic if you didn't take advantage of it. Just remember, if there's ever something on your videotape that you don't want, back it up and record over it.

This advice applies to other situations too. Most people seem to feel that since videotape is so cheap, they might as well save everything they've ever recorded. Now, this may sound bold, but we beg to disagree. There will be lots of times you'll be rolling tape when nothing very interesting is going on. Since you most likely won't be taking the time to sit down and edit these pieces out later, why not make the decision to edit them out now? Go ahead. Record over them. If you didn't get what you really wanted, and the piece is thirty seconds long or more, save your viewer some boredom and edit out that dull piece by recording over it. Remember, there's no sacred rule on the books that says everything you shoot is worth preserving forever. If you don't want it, record over it.

"I COULD KILL MYSELF" MISTAKE 3
ACCIDENTALLY RECORDING
OVER AN IMPORTANT TAPE

The worst stupid mistake you can make, next to letting your camcorder sink to the bottom of the ocean (and we'll get to that in a minute), is accidentally to record over something important. We call this a stupid mistake because that's exactly what everyone calls themselves when it happens to them. Fortunately, with just a little bit of foresight, this needn't ever to happen to you.

Your first safeguard is to be sure and label everything. It should never be too much trouble to make a quick label for each cassette and its case. And since we're discussing good habits, why not make an itemized list or log of what's on each tape too? Whenever you've finished recording on a tape, take a few minutes to sit down and fast scan through the entire thing. As you're scanning pause at each new section, write down what it's about, and include the tape counter numbers. Your finished log should look something like this:

DECEMBER 1988–JULY 1989

Darin's First Birthday 1988	0000–0560
Day at the Park	0560–0750
Easter Morning (Baskets)	0750–1020
Easter Egg Hunt	1020–1355
Trip to the Beach	1355–1430

Ten minutes of your time now will save you hours of aggravation later when you're trying to find that 1989 trip to the beach. Besides, this can be a very quick and pleasant way to view your entire tape at once. It's fun and the rest of your family will want to watch too.

The second safeguard is one of the simplest to use but one with which many people seem never to bother. On the back of every videocassette throughout the world is a plastic "Record Tab" whose sole purpose is to allow you to prevent anything from being recorded on that cassette. On 8mm cassettes it's a small slide switch that indicates red when it's in the "Safety" position. On VHS tapes it's a small plastic tab that needs to be physically broken off. Once you've activated either style of safety, a small sensor in your camcorder or VCR is notified that "this cassette should not be recorded on." Should you ever wish to record on one of these cassettes again, simply slide back the switch on the 8mm cassette or place a small piece of tape over the opening of the VHS cassette. By doing this you tell the sensor that it's okay to record and you're back in business again.

Another thought that can help you keep things more organized is to record on each cassette until it's completely full. Every event that you shoot doesn't need to be on a separate tape. It's wasteful and confusing to have a shelf full of tapes with only ten minutes of a birthday recorded on one and fifteen minutes of a swim trip on another. Besides, the fewer tapes you have lying around, the less chance you run of accidentally recording *The Beastmaster II* over a borrowed copy of your sister's wedding.

"I COULD KILL MYSELF" MISTAKE 4
DROPPING THE CAMCORDER

Nobody will want to be around you for a long time after you've watched your beloved video equipment fall smack onto the ground or plop into the deep blue sea. To say you'll be in a dark mood will be the understatement of the year.

There is one easy way to guard against something like this from ever happening: always avoid placing your camcorder in a precarious position. Sounds simple, doesn't it? All we're talking about are those common resting places like car tops or hoods, the ends of park benches, or on top of walls or fences. Remember, if it can happen, it will. Be forewarned and be careful.

The worst accident that can happen to your camcorder is to drop it into water. If this ever happens to you and you're lucky enough to rescue it before it sleeps with the fish, here's what you should do:

If you have dropped it into fresh water, like a fountain or lake, take the battery out and get it to a professional repair shop immediately. If you can get it there within a couple of hours of the accident, there's a good chance it can be saved.

If you have dropped it into salt water, the prospects will be less positive. There's only one rescue for a saltwater swim and that's to flush out your camcorder with fresh water immediately. Again, remove the battery as soon as possible, then rinse off the camcorder with fresh water. Once it's rinsed, grit your teeth because you need to go against common sense and immerse the whole thing again—this time, though, in a bucket or bag of fresh water. All of it, the entire camcorder, deep-sixed. Make sure it's *completely* covered with fresh water. The reason for this is that salt water starts acting as a corrosive almost as soon as it touches the electronics inside your camcorder. Your only hope for slowing this process down is to flush out as much of the salt water as possible, then keep any of the electronics from being exposed to air. Needless to say, you'll run, bag or bucket in hand, to the nearest camcorder repair facility. The odds will be less than fifty-fifty that your camcorder can be salvaged. Nevertheless, quick action by you will seriously improve the odds.

If you use your camcorder around open bodies of water, be careful. Keep that camera strap around your arm or neck at all times. Remember, as far as camcorders are concerned, a wet mistake is usually an expensive mistake.

CHECKLIST REVIEW FOR CRITICIZING YOUR OWN TAPES

Okay, we warned you at the beginning of this chapter that there would be a test. Well, here it is.

Your assignment is to pick one of your tapes, watch it, and do a critique for mistakes. Use the checklist just below to see how you stack up against our six most common mistakes. Don't be too hard on yourself, though. One or two mistakes in each category are perfectly acceptable. Only when you see a mistake being repeated over and over should you mark it down as an area that could use some improve ment. If you do have a problem area or two, take some time to review the tips we discussed, then get out your camcorder, put in a fresh tape, and practice. If you spend just one day practicing all of the tips, you will also have a fun "Day in the Life" tape of your family to show for it.

YOUR "COMMON MISTAKES" CHECKLIST

Remember, check a mistake only if you see it repeatedly in your videotapes. Once you've checked a mistake, write down what the solution would be, based on what you've learned in this section. Everyone is allowed to make any of these errors once or twice. But if a mistake is becoming a habit, review the solutions we have given you.

_____ Mistake: Camera moves that are too quick
                Solution: _____

_____ Mistake: Individual shots that are too long
                Solution: _____

_____ Mistake: Leaving your camcorder running
                Solution: _____

_____ Mistake: Shooting everything from one spot
                Solution: _____

_____ Mistake: Shooting when there's not enough light
                Solution: _____

_____ Mistake: Shooting where the backlight is too bright
                Solution: _____

3
LEARNING TO EDIT
AS YOU ARE
SHOOTING

BEFORE YOUR EYES start to glaze over and you begin to mumble, "I don't even know what editing is," hold tight. You may not realize it, but you do know what editing is. If you have grown up in the twentieth century (a fair assumption), you're one of those statistics who have watched twenty hours of television every week of their lives. You have seen "I Love Lucy," "Bewitched," "Happy Days," "Alf," "Cheers," "Night Court," and on and on and on. Every single hour you've watched on television, every single movie you've watched at the theater, has been edited. If the movies or TV shows hadn't been edited, they would appear as if they had been shot by a convenience store security camera. The shower scene in *Psycho* wouldn't look quite the same if Alfred Hitchcock had shot it in just one wide shot, would it?

Editing creates the pace and the excitement that suck you into a good movie. It can also enliven an otherwise dull sitcom or game show. In just one easy lesson, we will show you how to bring your home videos to life too. No longer will your videos look as if they belong in the 7-Eleven Hall of Fame. Just one endless shot, panning back and forth, zooming in and out, panning back and forth . . .

When we bring up the topic of editing, all we're really talking about is simply stopping the camera and changing the shot before you start rolling again. The same concept applies, no matter whether you're shooting a child's birthday on videotape or *Lawrence of Arabia* in 70mm Super Panavision. Every single shot is different from the one before and the one after.

What you're doing is enhancing the visual impact of a scene by choosing camera shots that complement each other. This may sound a little fancy, but your eye will recognize what works and what doesn't. And that, friends, is what it's all about. You are fooling your viewer's eye into thinking it is seeing what *it* wants, when actually you are the person selecting what it sees.

We will refer to this as editing within the camera, or editing as you are shooting. Actually editing is sitting down after you have finished shooting and selecting the best shots and the best angles, then rearranging them in the order that you decide. Not many of us have the time or even the desire to get into something like this. We don't and we suppose you don't either. So, we will teach you how to make your videos look as if you took the time to edit them when all you really did was stop tape and change position after each shot.

GOING TO EDITING SCHOOL

This will be the easiest school you have attended. You've been attending it most of your life but probably never noticed. The classroom is any seat in front of your television and it only has one rule: Learn by watching others. In fact, your homework assignment for tonight is to watch *anything* on TV and pay attention to the editing. It's okay to enjoy yourself, but watch the sequence of shots. You'll soon realize that you already do know quite a bit about editing. If anybody asks why you're wasting time watching TV, just answer, "Hey, I'm studying here!"

In its simplest form, editing consists of sequences of wide shots, medium shots, and closeups. The easiest way to edit these shots together is to arrange them in this same order.

"Editing" sequence:
(1) Tape a few seconds of a wide shot. Stop recording.
(2) Walk closer, change your position, and get a medium shot. Tape a few seconds, then stop recording.
(3) Zoom in for a closeup of the activity or of one participant. Record for a few seconds.

Use a wide shot to establish where your subjects are. This shot is as wide as your camcorder lens can shoot. It should show everything there is to see, either as one wide shot or as a pan shot that slowly reveals everything.

The medium shot acts as a transition between your wide shot and the closeup to follow. In its simplest form it is a shot that is zoomed in halfway between the wide shot and the closeup. It is tighter and closer to your subject than your wide shot was so it places a little more emphasis on what you feel is important.

A medium shot is very important simply because it is a transition. If you go from a wide shot to a closeup, without anything in between, your viewers will become disoriented. One second they see a wide shot of a backyard party, the next they see a closeup of somebody's face. Without a transition they will have no idea where that person is in the backyard or even whose face it might be.

A medium shot will begin to direct your viewers' attention to the area you think is important. If the wide shot reveals the entire backyard party, the medium shot will show the group of two or three people you feel are important. Once you've picked out a group, though, it's time to drive home your point with a closeup.

The closeup shot is where you get to shine as a creative artist. Here you decide what your viewer gets to see, because there's nothing else to look at. Fortunately, the whole world loves a closeup. You can't go wrong shooting closeups of faces, of hands working, of birthday cakes, of presents. It's the closeup shots that really bring your videos to life. Your viewers will get to see details that they otherwise would have seen only if they had been there. And after all, that's what you really want, isn't it? You want to capture that moment of being there.

While you're watching TV tonight notice that editing usually obeys one other rule. Each shot not only differs in size from the previous one, but usually differs in position too. When the professionals are filming a scene, they don't merely stop the camera, zoom in, then start rolling again. They also change the angle from where that next shot is taken. This is the second way to create interest, along with changing the size of the shot. The change in angle we're referring to doesn't have to be much, just enough to give a slightly different perspective to what you're shooting. Twenty or thirty degrees are plenty.

How you decide upon this change in position depends entirely

First shot is medium, full face to camera.

Second shot is closeup from the right.

upon how close you are to your subject. If you're close, within six feet, say, then you'll need to move only two feet or so to your left or right. If you're twenty or thirty feet away, then you'll need to move more, about eight feet either way.

This might be easier to understand if you imagine a clock face. If your subject is at the center of the clock, where the hands are, let's put you and your camcorder at the six o'clock position. Notice that we're using only half of the clock face. From nine o'clock to three o'clock, with you at six and your subject in the middle. If you have shot your first wide shot from six o'clock, shoot your medium shot from either seven or five. It doesn't matter which way you go. You can move to either your left or your right. What you're looking for is the side that

A wide shot from head-on.

A medium shot from a slightly different position.

**A closeup from an even different angle, but
still on the same side as the medium shot.**

will give you the best view of your subject. Once you have committed to moving right, you should stay to the right of six o'clock for the remainder of your shots of that subject. As soon as you move on to another subject, you're free to start the pattern over again.

You can watch this pattern develop while you're "studying" in front of the TV. Every show or movie works with the same pattern. After a while you might even be able to guess what the next shot will be. Maybe a well-edited movie will keep you guessing, but a typical sitcom will follow the same pattern over and over. People will move around in a wide shot. Once they stop moving the director will go to a medium shot as a transition. When there's a joke line you can almost bet that it will be in a closeup.

It's that simple. Three types of shots, mixed around and repeated endlessly. The professionals have directors and editors to do this for them. You have your camcorder and a start and stop button.

CREATING A SEQUENCE OF SHOTS

At its simplest, a sequence of shots can go like this:

★ Wide shot, stop tape.
★ Medium shot, stop tape.
★ Closeup, stop tape.

This pattern of shots worked very well for the early silent movies, but that was eighty years ago. In a way, you're following in their same footsteps. It took them a while to get past the basics and it might take you a little while too. If you're not too sure that you understand what we're getting at here, give it a try. Grab your camcorder and shoot some practice tape. As it is said in Hollywood, tape is cheap. Remember, you can always record over it.

Don't think that we've forgotten about the zoom lens either. Once the basic wide shot, medium shot, and closeup make sense to you, a whole new dimension waits to be opened with your zoom.

What you now have available to you is a way of making a smooth transition either from a wide shot to a medium, or from a closeup to a medium. Of course, there's no reason you can't zoom all the way from a wide shot to a closeup, or vice versa. It just looks better to only use a zoom to get you halfway; halfway out from a wide, or halfway in to a closeup.

If you decide to start your shot sequence with a wide shot, try zooming in to a medium, then stop tape. Change positions and change shot sizes, then roll tape again.

Try to avoid zooming from a wide shot to a closeup in one continuous shot. It's nearly impossible to make this type of move look decent, so try to avoid it altogether. Of course, there are exceptions to every rule. But we're not going to tell you any for this one. Full-range zoom? Just say no.

BUILDING EMPHASIS

The reason for learning to build a sequence of shots is to emphasize something that you have selected and decided is important to your viewer. There are several ways you can do this, but two of the best are the ten-second limit and reaction shots.

Ten-Second Limit

The ten-second limit is as simple as it sounds. Limit your shots to seven to ten seconds. That's it. In ten seconds your viewer's eye has had time to scan the entire picture and soak up all the areas of interest. If something is going on that takes more than ten seconds to cover, keep tape rolling. Otherwise, limit yourself to ten seconds. The "somethings" that might keep your tape rolling: someone finishing a conversation, a child riding a bike around the driveway, or a ballplayer rounding the bases after belting a home run. The only time you should shoot for longer than ten seconds is when you have made the conscious decision to keep rolling. Remember, ten seconds or less is usually best.

Reaction Shots

The other way to build emphasis is by reaction shots. A reaction shot is merely a two- or three-second glimpse of someone's face. By putting a couple of reactions into your sequence, you'll bring your viewers one step closer to being there. If they had been there, they would have been looking around at the other people. Since you are there, you should do the same. Everyone loves those closeups, so shoot plenty of reactions and you'll end up with the next best thing to being there.

KEY POINTS TO EDITING AS YOU SHOOT

1. The shots you select emphasize what *you* feel is important, and what isn't. In real life a person's eyes are constantly scanning and observing what's around them. When they watch a videotape, you help make these decisions for them.

2. Every time you start and stop your camera, you are editing. And every time you edit, you're momentarily increasing your viewers' level of attention. Their eyes quickly scan the shot for new areas of interest. Control this in an orderly sequence and you're directing their attention to the areas of interest you feel are the most important.

3. Direct your viewers' eye by building a logical sequence of shots. Start wide and work your way in to a closeup, or do it the other way around. Change the angle of your shot every time you stop the camera too. As long as you are shooting one subject, try not to let any two shots be the same. When you start on another subject, start the pattern all over again.

4. Keep your shots interesting by keeping them short. A good average length is seven to ten seconds. Start teaching yourself by silently counting to ten as you are shooting. Stop tape, move to another position, change frame size, then roll for another seven to ten. With a little practice you'll be able to stop tape and change position in five seconds. You'll also get better at picking out the natural pauses in action, and that will allow you to do all of this without missing anything important.

5. You cannot learn without watching. Watch television, watch movies, and always watch your own tapes with a critical eye. Look for what works and what doesn't. In your own tapes, watch for:

★ Moving too little or too far when you stop to change angles.
★ Picking a bad time to stop tape and move.
★ Changing shots from wide to closeup without a transition.

Learning to edit is both fun and easy. If you don't have the time to edit after you are finished shooting, teach yourself to edit while you are shooting. Your decisions won't always be perfect and you will make mistakes. But your videos will look much better than they would if you had done nothing more than stand-pan and zoom. You're not making a Hollywood feature so you shouldn't expect your end result to look like one. Follow the examples that we've given and keep adding new ones until they become second nature. Above all, watch others and keep learning. If you like an idea you see on TV, steal it.

Remember, there's nothing new under the sun and no rule that can't be bent—with a good reason, of course.

Part II
VIDEOTAPING
FAMILY LIFE

THIS IS THE PART of the book in which we try to persuade you that your everyday life is worth being videotaped. Yes, even the most mundane family activities have a place, somewhere, on some videotape. Before we start, though, we want to talk to you about something we feel is vital. From the many home videos we've seen it appears that most of our children live in houses by themselves, play at the park by themselves, take trips to amusement parks by themselves, and do all sorts of cute things—all by themselves. You can guess where we're headed here, can't you? These might be your children, but where are you on these videotapes?

You may think that you look too heavy, too old, or too tired (well, that may be true . . .), but you need to put vanity aside for the sake of your family videos. If you intend these videos to be a part of the legacy that you leave your children, they will want to see you in the videos too. Believe us, we're as critical of ourselves in photos and on video as anyone else, but it's crucial to realize how important it is to be seen on tape with your children. The natural joy and family interaction that you capture will far outweigh any of your own insecurities about how you may look. In the words of someone else's successful ad campaign, just do it.

4
VIDEOTAPING
THE KIDS

("Turn around, turn around"; "Sunrise, sunset"; etc., etc.)

OST OF THE PEOPLE we spoke with had bought their first camcorder to record their children's growth and development. Sitting down to watch the videos of our children's baby days, their school years, sporting events, holiday programs, and their daily life should be a favorite pastime for most doting parents. However, even with the best of intentions, parents can end up making their beloved children look terribly dull on tape.

The main reason for ending up with a BKV (Boring Kiddie Video) is—the camera operator. Yes, mom and dad, we mean you. Most of us, as parents, just don't know when to turn our camcorders off and we're even *more* guilty when it comes to our own children. Catching our child singing a favorite song may make for a charming video, but five to eight songs in a row moves quickly from charming to excruciating.

Yet these are exactly the types of tapes we all tend to stockpile and dislike watching. We know you're familiar with this scene: You're watching home videos with a group of people. The singing child part comes on. Everyone oohs and aahs—it's *so* cute. Then the second song starts. Then the third. The parent responsible for this video says, "Oh, she sings a couple more songs. . . ." People begin to get up and refresh their drinks or get a snack. By the fourth or fifth song, the guests' conversations are louder than the singing. Finally one of the parents says, "Well, let's just fast forward through some of this." There's a lesson to be learned from this—quit while you're ahead.

Invariably, the "fault" for pushing a video from the charming realm into the excruciating realm falls on the parent–camera operator. A child finishes singing or dancing or playing and the next thing you know a parent is urging the child to sing more, dance again, or play a different game. Once or twice is cute and fun. Five or six times are too much. Our personal contribution to this syndrome is all the footage we have of our daughter riding her bike in a circle in our yard. Why weren't two or three laps enough? What made us think five minutes of this would be fun to watch?

What you inevitably get when you urge your children on is a stagy video. It's not natural, the child doesn't look comfortable, and you won't get the spontaneous reactions that you want. Our children do so many wonderful and creative things—the goal is to capture the spontaneity of their play and the naturalness of their responses.

In light of the fact that *natural* seems to be the guiding thought in children's videos, here are a couple of techniques for catching the spontaneous play of your children:

Sneak up on them. That's right, sneak up on them. In all honesty, this is the way we have taped many of our most touching videos. If you hear your children playing in their room, if you hear your child reading a story out loud, if you notice your toddler is intensely trying to build a tower with blocks—sneak the camera out and begin shooting. Use your video equipment often enough and the sight of you in the doorway with the camcorder won't disrupt the activity.

If this is a truly precious moment you can even manage to get away with only hearing them sing or read and not seeing them. We did this when our toddler daughter was in her bedroom "reading" her favorite story. She was going page by page and giving a letter perfect recitation of the story, which she had memorized from the many times mom and dad had read the book. We thought that if she saw us with the camera, she'd stop reading the book aloud. So we stayed in the doorway, just out of sight. As we began recording we quietly identified what was going on, then just let the camera listen to the story for a short period of time. After the story was finished, we went into the room with the camera so we could see our daughter on camera. The fact that you might be shooting your video from around the corner doesn't matter as long as you capture the moment. And capturing the moment, even if it's just in sound, is a far better alternative than missing it entirely. Then your children will become used to it and won't alter their actions much when they do notice you're there.

Flattery will get you a great video. Everyone loves to be flattered. Whether toddlers or teenagers or adults, we love compliments and positive feedback. If you discover your children doing something that is new or that will make a cute video, flatter them. We can virtually guarantee that they will love to do it again.

The trick is to make the action look unprompted and fresh for the camera. May we suggest that you *don't* say, "That was really terrific. Do it again for the camera." This tends to blow the mood of whatever they were doing and encourage the mugging and antics that make up too many videos. Instead, say something like, "That was such a great story! Would you read it again for me?" Be sure that you say all of this before you begin recording. The on-camera prompts will get old after a while and definitely give your video an artificial look. On-camera cheers and verbal compliments, however, can be a very good way to end this particular type of video.

Your goal is to get natural actions and reactions on tape, not staged ones. To attain this, have a camcorder that's easily accessible and simple for you to use. And, again, use your camera enough that your children will remain at ease when they notice you're using it.

TIP

To get a more natural video of your children at play, don't call attention to yourself with the camera. Avoid off-camera cues such as, "Hey, we're taping now. Just keep playing." Instead, stay in the background of their play space and just use the camera to observe and record. Remember, we're not talking about fifteen minutes of this; maybe one minute or less, unless their activity dictates more time.

Now let's look at some of the areas we consider to be highly tape-able during the childhood years.

PREGNANCY, CHILDBIRTH, AND NEWBORN DAYS

Our first bit of advice here is to talk with each other about how much of your pregnancy, childbirth, and newborn days you want on tape. Try to come up with a realistic goal—and understand that you can always live with more or less, depending on what the whole experience is like. We don't mean that you should write up a video manifesto shortly after your pregnancy has been confirmed; just set up a framework for the pregnancy. Then, as you get closer to due date, come to an agreement about what you want to do during labor and delivery. At that time talk about what you really want to see once the baby is born. A little planning will help during what is, for all of us, an emotional time.

The marvelous thing about today's video technology is that we are the first generation that can record our growing family as life is beginning. Many obstetricians can even offer expectant parents a videotape of the fetal ultrasound. What a joy to have a video record of your first glimpse of your child! It is the miracle of life, a personal milestone for the parents-to-be, and the beginning of a new chapter in your family life. It's also the time to start thinking about buying a camcorder if you don't have one.

Pregnancy

Depending on how organized you are, you can either get extensive coverage of the pregnancy or merely hit the highlights. Of course, one person's highlights may be another's lowlights, especially if you're talking about the early, queasy stages of pregnancy. At the very least, we recommend getting some sort of videotape record of the pregnancy, maybe once or twice in each trimester to show the progressive growth of the woman's belly and a few comments about what's happening at that stage. A few "interview" questions may be all you need: Are you still queasy? Have you felt any movement yet? Do you think the baby has settled into position?

As the pregnancy progresses, you may wish to tape some of your preparations for the new baby. Is a room being redone for a nursery? Or are you moving things around to make room? If it isn't too probing, ask each other some questions about the pregnancy. Any apprehensions? Any thoughts about becoming a parent again, or for the first time? What kinds of thoughts are you having about the baby? Do you know the sex of the baby? How did you feel when you found out?

Most obstetricians will permit you to bring a video camera into the examining room as long as you've asked permission beforehand. Those monthly visits are usually very quick; the doctor usually checks only the fetal heartbeat and the growth of the baby. Getting at least one of the office visits on tape would be nice.

Childbirth

This is the part of your pregnancy video that must be discussed before it takes place. You surely will not be able to debate the merits of taping versus not taping during the actual labor.

Some questions you'll need to address:

★ How much of the labor and delivery do you want to tape?
★ Who will do the taping—the spouse/coach or a third person?
★ If the spouse/coach does the taping, how will you deal with his or her coaching responsibilities?
★ If a third party does the taping, when will you call that person? How can you make your expectations for this video understood by this person?

Because early labor with a first pregnancy can be lengthy, it should be fairly easy to tape one or two contractions. As the labor progresses, the woman might be less likely to want to participate in the taping process. However, you may have decided at an earlier date that you'd both like to get at least some of the heavy-duty labor on camera. If this has been decided and the woman is still cognizant of that fact when she is actually in labor, then the spouse should tell the woman that he's going to tape the next contraction. The woman can then say if she's okay with that, or if she really needs her spouse/coach with her.

T I P

It would be great to mark the passage of time periodically. You might start off your tape with a shot of the clock and give the date. Then every few hours come back to the clock and give an update on the timing between contractions. A final clock shot and voice-over before you leave for the hospital or birthing center would be a nice end to the early-labor stage.

As far as the delivery goes, we have mixed reports to offer. Surprisingly, many people we talked with had video cameras when their children were born, but opted not to tape the birth. The people who did tape the birth preferred, to a person, not to view that particular tape with any regularity. Most who taped the birth did so just "for the future," and the personal interest of their children. And that's fine. There is no need to justify a decision to tape or not tape your child's birth.

If you decide to tape the birth, the following four rules should guide you:

RULE 1. Get permission from the doctor beforehand. Most doctors permit video cameras in the delivery room as long as they know about it first.

RULE 2. Be realistic about how difficult it will be to be both the coach and the camera operator. Labor does get intense, to say the least, and even the woman who previously wanted step-by-step documentation might find that making a videolog of labor is the last thing on her mind when she is feeling those contractions. Go into it with an ideal plan that you know will be amended during the labor and delivery. Also, consider having a friend or relative do your taping for you.

RULE 3. If you are having a third person tape the delivery, make your wishes as clear as possible beforehand. As you know, labor and delivery are an unpredictable experience within a predictable framework, so your camera operator needs to know that she might be called in the middle of the night, or even while at work. As coach, you can certainly talk with the camera operator while the whole event is under way, but you probably won't have the presence of mind also to direct videos when you're in the middle of coaching the "Hee, Hee, Hee, Hoo's."

RULE 4. Don't get in the way of the medical professionals who are delivering the baby. The obstetrician or nurses will direct the camera operator on where to stand. The camera operator will not be allowed to stand within the "sterile field," which is the area surrounding the woman's lower half. That fact may make you more comfortable with having a third person (besides the nurses, aides, and doctors) in the delivery room.

The main reason, to us, for taping the childbirth is to capture that emotional, euphoric high that comes from bringing a new life into the world. After all, you're not trying to make a graphic medical tape. You are trying to record the work, the sweat, and the love that go into every baby brought into this world.

The camera operator's attention should be directed at the mother-to-be and her coach or coaches. Get medium and closeup shots of everyone's face; emphasize what is happening above the waist, not below. When the new addition arrives, keep tape rolling. Follow the baby wherever it goes—from the doctor to the nurse to the mom or dad. Pay special attention to the mother too. There will be lots of tears and kissing going on and this is the love and emotion you really want to catch. Because there will be all sorts of background noises, try to get as close to the new parents as possible so that their comments are clearly picked up. Be sure to record some tight closeups of that seconds-old newborn face. These are those wonderful once-in-a-lifetime memories that we keep talking about.

One person we spoke with told us what she thought was the "best part" of her baby's birth video. The person taking the video followed the newborn and recorded the Apgar Test each time it was administered. This series of five tests, given at one minute and again at five minutes after birth, records the coordination and level of responses that all newborns have. The camera operator also followed the baby and nurses into the newborn nursery where the pediatrician checked the baby and the nurses bathed the infant. The woman who told us of this said that even though she couldn't bring herself to watch the actual birth portion, she was fascinated with this "aftercare," which she was unable to see for herself. Our unofficial poll of women we know who have had children found that they, too, would have loved to see those first checkups.

Although we chose not to tape our second child's birth (we didn't have a video camera when the first was born), we did take the camera to the hospital. We taped something that, to us, captured the wonder of this new life and the pure sweetness of our tiny baby. The baby was sleeping in his hospital bassinet. All we did was focus on him, close up, and begin recording. We quietly identified the scene, specifically that he was nine hours old, and just let the tape roll. We stayed on this shot for maybe four minutes. Now, four minutes of a baby sleeping may sound like a long time, but what we got on tape were all the little squeaks, the facial expressions, and the head movements of our sleeping angel. This scene is what his grandparents and relatives loved the most. We think we like it so much just because of its simplicity. In the excitement of the new baby—the hospital guests, the homecoming—it's nice to get something of the newborn's simple joys and needs.

If the mother is to be in the hospital for a few days, it might be a good idea to leave the camcorder with her. Please don't think that we're suggesting that the new mom jump into a Superwoman role. Go through labor! Go through delivery! Get that baby in the room and make a movie! With our first baby (when we didn't have a camcorder) we doubt that we could have been very focused on making videos, because we were in such a fog after the birth. With our second, though, we were more psychologically prepared for the whole event and were able to know that we would treasure more photos and certainly more videotape of the baby's first days. So if it's possible, keep the camcorder close to the hospital bed. That way, if things are going well, mom can shoot scenes of the baby asleep and the newborn's squeaks and cries.

Homecoming and Newborn Days

If this is *not* your first child, we wouldn't recommend keeping the camera at the hospital for the duration of the stay. The reason is, you'll want to have some videos of the siblings at home preparing for the arrival of mom and the new baby. Things might be crazy at home, but a fun way to start the homecoming video is to give a tour of all of the preparations that have been made. If you do have other children, let them give the tour—point out the baby's bed and clothes, how the house has (or hasn't) been cleaned. Ask the children what they think the new baby will want to "do" first and "see" first, and what mom will be surprised to see.

If this is your first child, then dad should make the video. Remember, this video will record the last prebaby look at your house or apartment—life will never be quite the same. If you have a friend or relative at home to help out with the new one, ask that person a few questions about the baby: Is this your first grandchild? Are you anxious to hold the newborn? Does holding a new baby bring back any special memories?

When you're back at the hospital (or birthing center), shoot some of the mother's room—packages, flowers, general disarray. Then, if the baby isn't already dressed, get some of that on tape too.

If an attendant arrives with a wheelchair, record some of the start of the trip, then try to tape again once you've reached your car. It's fun to see your little treasure all strapped and fitted into that enormous infant car seat. When you arrive home, tape the mother and child entering the house for the first time. Try to tape as much as you can without affecting the reality of the situation. This is one of those times when precise balancing on that tightrope between documenting and participating is crucial.

A tip we got when we had our second child was to let someone else carry the newborn into the house so that the mother would be free to give some attention to the older child or children. This seems like a good idea, and can even allow mom to make some videos of dad and the newborn.

If this is not your first child, certainly include your other children in the tape of the new baby's first days. "Interview" them as to their feelings about the new baby. If there's even a hint of jealousy, avoid questions like: Do you love the baby already? Isn't the baby so sweet? and ask those lighter in tone: Do you think the new baby will like spaghetti as much as you do? What do you think the new baby will like best about you? What do you think the baby dreams about when she is sleeping?

Newborn Days

Some of the nicest videos we shot of our newborn baby were spinoffs of our hospital baby sleeping videos—a grandparent holding the baby, mother nursing the baby, the bundled baby sleeping. With only an identifying voice-over (date, how old the baby was), we simply shot a minute's worth or less of each activity during those special first days.

A fun idea is to emphasize how tiny the baby is. Lay the infant on the bed next to one of dad's socks or shoot a closeup of an older sibling's hand with the newborn's hand. The baby grows so fast that we quickly forget how small the newborn was.

You may think we're crazy when you read this next idea, but here goes. As you parents know, those first days, weeks, and, face it, months of life with your new baby are marked by your own loss of sleep. Whether the baby is up every two or three hours, or miraculously sleeps for five hours straight, you tend to focus on how much sleep you didn't get. If you have older children, you know that those first weeks seem endless when you're experiencing them, but they soon pass. Why not get some of that exhausting routine on tape? You're up anyway; you might as well do something.

Pick a night, any night, and keep the camcorder close at hand. When the baby wakes and you're both roused from sleep, whoever isn't caring for the baby should make a recording. Once again, don't do it in "real time"—we're not looking for a ten- to twenty-minute video. In your drowsy voice give the time, date, and what's happening: "It's almost midnight, July second, and this is the first feeding. We're changing a diaper and then we'll head for the couch." The next scene should begin when mother and baby are settled and feeding. Less than a minute of the feeding should be sufficient. If you're not too self-conscious about it, try to get a shot from the mother's point of view. Shoot a closeup of the baby nursing from over the mother's shoulder. This is a view she'll see many, many times and it's special enough to serve as a precious memory for years to come. The last shot should be of the contented, sleeping baby back in the cradle or crib. Place the camcorder by your bed and go to sleep. When the baby wakes again, repeat the taping procedure. If you're experiencing a particularly bad night with many feedings, you'll definitely wonder why you're making this tape. However, these middle-of-the-night feedings won't last forever and unless you capture it on videotape, the memory of holding that precious little bundle in semidarkness in the quiet house will soon fade too.

INFANCY AND TODDLER YEARS: IMPORTANT FIRSTS

Like most parents, we made a valiant attempt to record every possible first in our babies' development. Having gone through this, we would advise that you don't set yourself up to fail; no matter how hard you try you will not get *every* first developmental hurdle on tape. If recording as much as possible of your child's first year is a high priority for you, get as much as you can when you can—your baby rolling over will look the same the second day as the first. You will be thrilled to see it on tape regardless of when you recorded it.

Is it possible to tape too much of the first year of your child's life? We don't believe so. Just know that you probably are going to have a lot of redundant tapes, but this year of infancy is something that, obviously, will never happen again. You should tape according to these guidelines, though: limit the length of your shots; identify the date, location, and age of the baby; and always think beginning, middle, and end to your pieces.

T I P

Just as you should always keep your still camera handy and loaded with film, do the same with your camcorder and try keeping it in your baby's bedroom. If this is your first child, you don't need to worry about other siblings getting into the equipment. If you do have other children, keep the camcorder out of their reach but still in the baby's room. The camera then is near the center of action and you can quickly reach it whenever a golden moment occurs.

An Idea for Your Toddler

One of the greatest things about being a toddler is that everything is new. Toddlers suddenly obtain access to a whole new level of exciting things to explore. For mom and dad, these months are spent being completely and utterly in adoration of their little one and being scared out of their minds about the dangers of hardwood floors, sharp corners, open toilet seats, and errant kitchen utensils.

Since your toddler most likely won't sit still while there are things to explore, why not follow your child around, at her eye level? Now, you won't do this for an entire day. Just pick a time, any time, and follow that kid around. Begin the video by identifying location, date, age of the child, and activity: "We're going on an Annelise-sized exploration of the kitchen." For the next three or four minutes (or depending on when your knees give out) follow the child while holding the camera approximately at her eye level.

Be sure to zoom in close to whatever the child has picked out as an enthralling find, even if it is only the lid to a plastic bowl. Remember, you've joined the world of a toddler. Depending on how verbal your child is, you might ask questions; or merely let the natural sound fill the video. The idea of camera-as-observer is one that deserves some experimentation. That is, try not saying anything for a while and just let the camera observe and record your toddler's developmental breakthroughs.

Remember to vary your shots. Stop taping, change your position, change the type of shot, and begin recording again. The video might end as the toddler gets up and walks away from the first area of interest; or if you sense that you have enough on tape; or if your knees and back just can't take any more crouching. If your tape does not have a visual end—like the child leaving the room—make sure that you end it with a voice-over like, "Well, that's it for exploring in the kitchen."

CHILDHOOD

This tends to be the time when we haul out the camera only for special occasions—birthdays, holidays, vacations—which we'll address in Part III. Although the newness of our children has worn off and we've jumped into the frenetic routine of raising them, the miracle of watching children grow never leaves us. The childhood years are definitely the time to have an easy-to-handle camera available; things tend to happen so quickly that if you have to think twice about hauling out equipment, you won't do it.

Your goal should be to accumulate a good library of your child's early years. By documenting your children you're recording your family's life as well. It's personalities you want on tape and if you're consistent, you'll be able to view the essence of the adult your child will become.

Change your taping mindset from thinking only of taping special occasions to taping minor events too:

★ If we're talking preschooler, tape some of your child coloring in a book.
★ Ask preschoolers to introduce you to their favorite toys.
★ Maybe the child is writing the alphabet for the first time; if so, grab the camera and shoot some video.
★ Has your child finally mastered the somersault? Tape it.
★ How about taping that first homework assignment?
★ Can your child finally make his own bed?
★ Does your child have a favorite TV show? Tape a few minutes of the child watching it, and ask why the show is a favorite.

★ Has your child had a bad day? Ask her to talk about it on tape, so you can all keep track and see if things get better.
★ Does your child have a favorite book? Tell us about it.
★ Do your children have a particular game that they like to play together? Have them explain it; then tape some of it.
★ And don't forget family pets. They're part of childhood memories. So get some tape of the children with their animal (or reptile) friends.
★ Ask your children to tell you why they admire a particular sports hero.
★ Have your children sit down. Then ask them to tell you what they like most about each other, and what frustrates them most about each other. (Do this with friends too.)
★ Ask your children what they think is the most important event in the news.
★ Has your adolescent made his room his private domain? Ask for a guided tour of the posters and mementos.

We hope you get our point. Be creative about how you use your camera and when. The idea is to make the camera such a normal part of life that you're able to get natural reactions on tape.

TIPS TO REMEMBER

Think closeups. Earlier we addressed the fact that some people tend to shoot everything in wide and medium shots. If you are taping a sequence of your child at play, be sure to get closeup shots. It is the innocence of that childhood face you will want to remember.

Think natural, everyday actions. Don't limit yourself by thinking that you should record your beloved children on only their best behavior and only on special occasions. They don't have to be dressed in their finest clothes, either. What you should be aiming for in your body of work is a glimpse of what your children, collectively and as individuals, were like during their childhood years. If all you shoot are stiff holiday portraits of children looking ill at ease in new dress-up clothes, you will have well posed videos with little emotion. A few backyard tussles, cranky outbursts, messy rooms, and romps in mudpuddles will add color to your video library.

Let the kids use the camera. As soon as you can safely allow it, let your children do some taping. One way to incorporate your video camera into your everyday life is to teach everyone how to use the equipment. We are well aware that, after you have taken great care to make good videos, your children will shoot some pretty messy pieces. But they have to learn even as you had to, so don't be overly critical. If you're concerned about ruining what you think is a fairly decent video, put in another tape and label it so you will all know that it is for the kids to use in their experimentation. Remember, your children will copy what they've seen you do. So if you have set a creative example, your children will likely pick up the ball and run with it. We'll address more techniques and ideas in Chapter 8, but for now, let us simply suggest that you get your children started by taping around the house, their friends at play, and their siblings. Definitely give them a turn with the camera on holidays and special occasions. And, very important, let them take videos of you. It will be fascinating to see what part of your life your child chooses to tape.

A final word. Your goal should be to accumulate a library of your children and their actions, good and bad. To get natural reactions on tape, the children must be used to seeing the video equipment in use. They need to know that the camera is merely observing and recording and that it is a friend. This means that you, as camera operator, must make the experience of being videotaped fun. If you begin to play the role of director—and dictator—once you pick up that camera, you're not going to see many happy children at play. Think of the camera as observing the activity and not as interfering in it.

Keep it all in perspective. If you fail to get the cute reaction or comment you want, don't get angry at yourself or frustrated with your child. Just wait for the next time.

5

SINGLE-PARENT AND BLENDED-FAMILY VIDEOS

T'S A FACT OF LIFE these days that our families will most likely be touched by divorce. We hope it won't happen in your immediate nuclear unit, but statistics show that somewhere in your extended family someone will be facing the issue of divorce and blended families. So what do you do about your videos? How do you keep your fun family outlook when your version of family doesn't fit neatly into a mom-dad-children mold? We think the answer is—keep making those videos.

Just because you are separated or divorced doesn't mean that birthdays don't mean as much to your kids and that holidays aren't as important. In fact, it may be even more important for you to record your celebrations to show the children that life goes on. Your family life is changing but everything has a way of working out.

SINGLE-PARENT VIDEOS

Being a single parent doesn't mean that participating and documenting become an either-or proposition. It's important to keep making videos but it's even more important to be a part of whatever is going on. You need to be there helping to open presents at Christmas or walking out with the birthday cake. To make all of this happen you'll need a tripod. By mounting the camcorder on a tripod you'll be able to tape the event and participate in it at the same time.

Of course, your friends and relatives are also very important. Extra help can run the birthday party while you videotape. Or you can enlist a friend or relative to do all the taping while you enjoy the children's activity. If you don't have another person to help out, settle for the tripod shot. The resulting static shot isn't ideal, but it's not the worst thing in the world either. Until your children are old enough to share in using the camcorder, a tripod may be your best home video friend.

You may also be well served by getting a smaller, more compact video camera. If it's just you and the children, you'll have a hard time lugging around a lot of extra video equipment. The smaller, palm-size models will probably work best for you.

To understand how you can tape a birthday party with just one camera operator and a tripod, read on.

TAPING A BIRTHDAY PARTY WITH ONE CAMERA OPERATOR

First of all, put some time into planning where the birthday party will take place. We suggest two locations—one for the overall party, the other for the cake and food. Then determine a place for your camera tripod in both locations. Have the tripod set up for the beginning of the party in the general location, then just before you call the children to the table for the cake, move the tripod to the food location.

Next, decide what must be on tape. Bringing out the cake? Opening presents? Party games? Plan for what you see as the essentials, and accept anything else as a bonus. Here's a technique which is also used in taping holidays:

★ set up the camera
★ tape for three to five minutes
★ stop recording for ten to fifteen minutes
★ repeat the cycle

Remember, you're aiming for highlights of the party, not the whole thing.

On the day of the birthday party get some hand-held shots of the birthday child. As you would in any other birthday video, ask the child what's special about the day, what needs to be done to set up for the party, if she's excited, etc. Once that's done, prepare for the party.

Party Time

Just before party time pan the scene of the party—the decorations, the birthday child all dressed up and anxious. Then put the camera on the tripod in the party area and frame up a wide shot. As guests arrive, explain that you will be taping periodically, and ask the children to help out by not playing close to the camera.

When most of your guests have arrived, turn on the camera and glance at your watch. After three or four minutes, turn the camera off. Depending on how long the prefood time lasts, every fifteen minutes or so walk over and turn the camera on. If party games are taking place, certainly let the camera record a little longer to get the action.

Do not feel that the camcorder must stay on the tripod all the time. If opportunities arise when you are able to break away for a minute or two, take the camera off and shoot some videos yourself. If possible, let a parent or helper supervise the party for a moment while you grab a few closeups of the birthday child.

Position the tripod and camera so that your wide shot covers the entire play area.

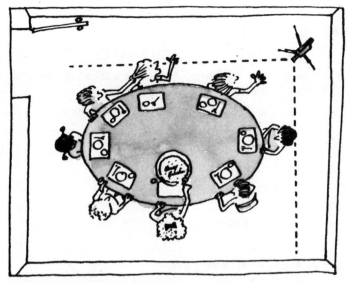

Keep the birthday child centered in your shot and include as many other guests as you can.

Cake Time

Shortly before you call the children for cake, move the camera and tripod over to its preset spot by the table. Depending on how long the camcorder has been running, you may want to put in a fresh battery. As soon as you're set up call the children over. Once the children are seated, take a moment to check the camera and make sure that you have an unobstructed view of the birthday child. Once again, let the other children know what you're doing and scoot people around in order to get a good picture. Begin recording. Bring the cake out and sing. When the candles have been blown out and the revelry has died down, walk over and stop recording.

Presents

Next come the presents. Move the camera and tripod back to their party location. Gather the presents around the child and again, check your shot to make sure that the birthday child is centered in the picture. Remember, you're after only highlights of the party. You don't need to see your child unwrap every present, so turn on the camera occasionally, for perhaps three minutes maximum. If you record two or three scenes of presents being unwrapped, those will be enough.

End of Party

For a final shot of the party, ask the guests to gather round the birthday child and say "Happy Birthday!" This will provide a beautiful ending for your tape. If you have been diligent in your recording, you'll have scenes of every part of the party, and a nice memory. After the party is over, you can get some more hand-held shots of the birthday child and comments about the party—maybe some shots of the child and her siblings playing with the new toys. Although it wasn't easy, now you have the best of both worlds—birthday party videos and a day spent participating with your child.

BLENDED-FAMILY VIDEOS

The blended family adds a new twist to fun family videos. Even though the adjustment period for the new family may not be smooth sailing, it's important to continue making videos. Making the videos and getting the holidays and everyday life on tape will be a concrete sign to all concerned that this is a new family, creating a new-family foundation and life together.

In fact, you may find it wise to use your camcorder to help the new siblings interact. Why not let the older children take the camera and create their own video? Using some of our ideas from Chapter 8, you could encourage the kids to act out a current film, or a favorite television show or book. Or, ask the older children's assistance in planning the birthday coverage for a younger child.

It also helps to watch a lot of family videos. Children love to see themselves acting silly and love to relive the excitement of birthdays and holidays. Viewing the new-family videos together can help cement that family bond.

Now this next idea may require extra fortitude on your part, but we feel you should also allow your older children to take the video camera when they visit the parent they don't live with. You should encourage your children to record life from their perspective—and their perspective happens to include life with your ex-spouse. If this is really a problem for you, why not let your children devote a special tape to the holidays or periods of time that they spend with their other parent? In that way, they can easily grab the tape and play it when they want to.

You also might end up dealing with children, an ex-spouse, and one camcorder. If this is your predicament, it would be nice if you could share custody of both the children and the camcorder. Whoever has the children at the moment should also have access to the cam-corder. This way you'll still be able to cover those special moments and keep doing what is best for the children. If they're spending every other weekend with dad, the camcorder should accompany them. This doesn't mean that mom or dad has to use the equipment every other weekend, but now it will be there just in case, as it was when everyone lived under one roof.

None of this will be easy for you, but if you're already going through any of these experiences, you're well aware of the life-isn't-always-easy speeches. Try to keep in mind the goal of recording your children's lives. This upheaval doesn't mean that you should have a two-year chunk of time with no birthdays, no holidays, no family life recorded. Once again, continuing to tape your changing family life will most likely help your children adjust to the changes they are facing. Emphasize fun and the joy your children bring to you.

6
EVERYDAY LIFE

MAJORITY OF PEOPLE with camcorders, it seems, never tape any of their daily routine; they use their video equipment only for holidays, birthdays, and other special occasions. Special events are fine, but life is lived day by day and the routine of your family is what will flavor your children's memory of their childhood years. We feel that although the idea of taping everyday life is unusual for most people, this is the kind of tape people will especially cherish in their later years.

When you think back to your own childhood, what memories stand out in your mind? Sure, you remember certain holidays and some fun vacations, but if you're like us, what you remember is just the essence of your childhood. And what makes up that essence are all the little and inconsequential events of daily life, such as dad always sitting in one chair and reading the paper, mom disappearing into the kitchen around five to begin supper, either of them rustling you out of bed in the morning to prepare for school. This is the stuff you tend to describe as: "My mother always used to do that"; "Dad always did it that way." As the years drift by, the details of that life fade and what remain are a few images and some vague recollections of times past.

Remember, right now you're in the process of giving your own children those types of memories. The wonderful part about it is, now you can record a slice of this ordinary daily life on tape.

We've come up with some guidelines that may make it easier for you, especially if you've never taped anything like this before.

What you're making is a documentary of family life. The events to catch are those that people do naturally, not posed shots or closeups with the off-camera command to do something.

So begin with the basics. Think of your family's daily routines—getting the kids up and ready for school, meal preparation, household chores, after-dinner habits. Now you don't have to cover these events in real time, meaning that you turn on the camera and let it run for the duration of the routine. Like taping anything else, you should tape for a few seconds, turn off the camera, move to a new location, tape a few seconds more, etc. What you're aiming for is the essence of the event.

There are two ways to do this type of taping: (1) as an observer, (2) by interacting with the subjects. If you, as the camera person, are not participating in the routine but merely following the action as it unfolds, you are observing the event. If, as the camera person, you question your family members about what's going on, you're creating an interactive video. Neither type is better than the other; it's purely up to you. Each type has a different feel and is nice to watch. We saw a really lovely moment on a tape—a grandmother and her three-year-old granddaughter making a pie. The camera operator did not say a word throughout the piece. All we could hear was the conversation between grandmother and granddaughter. The whole scene was probably five minutes long. It was a pleasant moment. We also saw a nice piece in which the camera operator and his relative discussed the relative's house, which was under construction. We saw closeups of blueprints, shots of what probably would be walls, doors, etc., during which a conversation went on between operator and subject. It was fun to watch.

If you've never done anything like this it's wise to start small. At first you will find it nearly impossible to figure out a routine to tape, so keep the camera handy for a few days. Do you see your oldest child and spouse in the kitchen doing the dishes? Grab the camera and tape the scene. How about the kids sitting at the table, using their watercolors? Or someone helping to take out the trash cans on trash day? After a couple of tries, people will begin to ignore the camcorder and go on with their tasks.

A SLICE-OF-LIFE TAPE

Evening meal preparation and eating are usually easy places to start if you can't think of anything else. Even the most frazzled people usually have some sort of routine at suppertime. Remember, you're not going for an hour-and-a-half tape, just highlights.

★ Begin the piece by identifying what we're watching; give the date too.
★ We should see some food being chopped up, seasoned, or otherwise prepared.
★ Next, shoot a little of the cooking.
★ Is someone setting the table? Record some of that too.
★ Who's pouring the drinks for everybody?
★ Now tape some of the food coming from the oven or stove (or how about the beep-beep-beep that signals the microwave is finished?).
★ You'll of course want to capture the herding of the little ones into the bathroom to wash hands, and the effort to corral them into sitting down.
★ Once the meal is ready, you will probably want to eat with your family. You can either stop taping once everyone is set to eat, or put the camera on a tripod with a locked wide shot. If you choose the latter, don't forget to turn the camera off after a few minutes. Remember, all you're after is the flavor of the routine.
★ You may want to finish the tape with a shot of family members clearing the dishes.

Now, are you still wondering why we would encourage you to tape something like an ordinary, everyday meal? Well, view your tape of the supper you just shot.

★ You've got your family preparing a meal that you'll remember as one of your favorites.

★ You see the three-year-old using the teddy-bear cup he couldn't live without.
★ You hear your daughter chattering happily about pouring the milk without spilling a drop.

You are watching a slice of life and we'll bet money that you'll be glad you grabbed the camera that one evening among thousands of evenings of meal preparations.

Listen, you're reading a book by two people who still kick themselves that they didn't tape the first running of the new dishwasher. It's not that we're so incredibly dull, but that it was an important milestone in our lives; the way we all jumped around and cheered when the darn machine started, we should've had it on tape.

"A DAY IN THE LIFE OF . . ."

When our first child was born we began using the "Day in the Life of . . ." concept to share the baby's days with our families, neither of which lived near us. To the best of our abilities, we've tried to keep up with this annually. The idea is to follow one child around for an entire day, from waking up in the morning to turning the light out at night. We're *not* talking about a twelve- or fourteen-hour tape. Ours usually run about forty-five minutes—about the length that any person can watch home videos in one sitting.

What you're aiming at is taping snippets of things as they happen. You don't need breakfast, lunch, snacktime, and dinner taped in their entirety. You just need to show that each meal took place. Pick a day that you suppose will be an ordinary day with perhaps one or two ordinary things going on. It should not be a day in which something extraordinary has been planned.

How to Tape "A Day in the Life of . . ."

★ The night before, check the video camera for tape and batteries. Leave the camera out, or even in your bedroom, so you can grab it when you first hear the child waking up.
★ Throughout the day, tape perhaps one to four minutes of each activity.
★ Take the camera with you as you run your errands, recording the child's participation.

★ Tape perhaps a minute of activity during each mealtime, something representative of that routine.

★ Periodically show a clock so that we can see that time is passing; or at least make sure that you voice-over the time once in a while.

★ Follow your child through the bedtime routine. Once again, a minute or less of each activity, unless there's a conversation going on or you want to capture the activity in its entirety.

★ Be sure to record the bedtime story or prayers and final tuck into bed.

★ Your final shot should be of lights out and last good nights.

Remember, this is one child's day, so the focus should be on that child. The routines of the day should be from the child's perspective. For example, the child accompanies you to pick up the dry cleaning. With the camera running, you might say, "Well, we just picked up the dry cleaning. Timmy, what do you think about it?" Timmy might reply, "I'm hot and I want to go home." Or, "I like it when the clothes go around and around on the racks." Then you might respond, "Okay, we did our errand, let's go home." And that's it for that scene in the tape.

Taping a "Day in the Life of" takes total commitment for a day but, believe us, the results are fun to watch. If nothing else, you'll pat yourself on the back for all that you do in a typical day. It's exhausting.

And don't think that you have to get everyone on his best behavior. If siblings start to bicker or if someone snaps at someone else, just put it down as a typical day. We even have one "Day in the Life of" tape that shows how best laid plans can go awry. Although it was to be just an ordinary day, as it turned out, nothing went right for us. By midday we were all snapping at each other and by the end of the day we couldn't do a thing without something going wrong. As time goes by, the tape's comic appeal grows because it clearly captures the tribulations of one family's ordinary Saturday.

Now, as we do it, a "Day in the Life of . . ." focuses on one child. If you have more than one child, you'll need to help the children understand that they will all have their day as stars of the show. You must be very dedicated and not let weeks and weeks pass before the other children do get their day. To begin, though, you may want to do a "Day in the Life of . . ." with your family as the subject. That might be easier if you've never tried this before.

If you end up enjoying this approach, you might try recording "A Day at Work," or "A Day at School." At the very least, we've always wanted to get some video of our drive to work. Not because it's exciting, but because the freeways and the routes we take have been an integral part of our work lives.

Videotaping at the office will certainly require the cooperation of your boss. We recommend that you consider videotaping at least *some* elements of your workday because they may be of interest to your children when they're older. Once again, think back to your own childhood; you probably know what your father's and mother's professions were, but are you certain about what they did at their place of work? What did their work space look like? Who were their friends at work? What were their normal work routines? Your children might ask the same questions of your work.

As far as "A Day at School" goes, I'm sure that you'd have a hard time convincing a teenager to let mom or dad follow him around for a day with a video camera. We've all been teenagers before and know how that thought would have mortified us. However, if your older child is proficient with the camera, perhaps let him take the camera for a day and tape his own school routines.

For younger children, those not yet completely embarrassed by the presence of their parents, the idea of having mom or dad with them for a portion of their day might be exciting. We taped a morning of our son's toddler room at the day-care center and the results were quite cute. It was fun to see how the little children interacted, how bold they were on the playgrounds, how snugly they were with the teachers and aides. The children easily got used to a dad being in the room, walking around with the camera. Our video ended when it was lights out for afternoon naptime.

VIDEO CHAIN LETTERS

Once you have mastered the "Day in the Life of . . ." approach, try having some fun with it. Remember, we started this type of taping because our families did not live near us. If you're in the same boat, why not merge the "Day in the Life of . . ." with the video chain letter? Send your "Day in the Life of . . ." to relatives. They will view it, then dub their own "Day in the Life of . . ." to yours, and send to the next relative, who will do the same thing. This is a great way for families to remain in touch. You're all sharing a slice of your everyday lives with one another.

We talked to someone who kept a video chain letter going with high school friends. On receiving the video, each person added on a five- or ten-minute piece about something in her life—showing friends around the new house, taping the baby who just learned to crawl, and the like. We think this idea is charming if for no other reason than it gives you yet another option, beyond writing and phoning, for maintaining relationships.

With some planning, you can make a video chain letter into a thoughtful gift for parents or grandparents. Make a video chain letter of the grandchildren for a special gift. For a special anniversary gift, have relatives and friends participate in offering their on-camera memories of the couple.

If you decide to try one of these more involved video letters, here are a couple of pointers:

★ Type up a basic form that all the participants should loosely adhere to. Set a ballpark time for each segment—maybe five minutes. Depending on how many people you'll have participating and how at ease people are with the video camera, five to ten minutes should be a good average time.

★ Since all participants will be adding their video memories to the same tape, ask that everyone follow a basic formula of letting the tape run for three or four seconds before starting to record. Those few seconds between each piece will protect against recording over the previous segment.

To sum up, we hope we've persuaded you that recording everyday life once in a while can add pleasant and poignant memories to your videotape library. If you have never done anything like this before, start small, with perhaps a mealtime routine or an evening routine. Then try "A Day in the Life of . . ." and see if you don't get hooked on making minidocumentaries of your family life. These tapes may be not so much for you as for your children, and for those times down the road when they and their children come to visit. It will be nice to remember those days among so many ordinary days that helped make up one of the best times of your life.

7
VIDEO AS HISTORY: RECORDING YOUR FAMILY'S ROOTS

OR SOME OF US, it takes having our own children to know and appreciate the importance of our immediate and extended family. Once you become a parent yourself, you look back at the sacrifices made by your own parents and you reflect on the decisions they had to make. You think of your grandparents and their lives, and you begin to see your own place in the story of your particular family.

While we were researching this project, several people told us that they were grateful they had taped a grandparent or other relative before that person passed away. That tape now possessed added emotional value and the fact that the person was no longer here made the tape priceless. Other people voiced the fact that though they liked taping their elderly relatives, what they ended up with was, typically, a shot of one of them in a chair or on a couch with a voice-over like, "And here's Aunt Mabel."

It's nice to see someone on tape, but when your child asks you about Aunt Mabel, wouldn't you like to have something more to say than "Oh, she was grandpa's sister"? Most of the older people in anyone's family have a story to tell, and their story is part of what put you where you are today. With some planning and your trusty video equipment in tow, you have the capability to make your own family saga for all to see.

Recording something like a family history takes a lot of effort. You have to want to do it, and you have to plan for it. You must think ahead enough to take advantage of interview opportunities. The payoff of all this effort is a visual history of the people in your immediate and extended family.

SETTING UP THE PROCESS

If every member of your immediate and extended family lives near you, taping a family history may take only a couple of months. If, like many of us, you have very few family members living nearby, working on this project is something you'll do piecemeal over a few years. Don't be put off by "years." After all, many of our cinematic geniuses took years to see their projects through to completion. You should develop a method for interviewing and at least an outline of what you'd like the finished product to look like. But, even if your finished tape contains only interview after interview, pat yourself on the back for making the effort to record your roots.

Most important: Set aside a master tape. This should be a tape of the highest quality you can buy. What you should do is tape your interviews and then dub them onto the master tape. Keep this tape in a safe location. It wouldn't hurt to make a couple of copies of the master tape and keep them in separate locations.

Next, do some preproduction. Make a list of whom you would like to interview. Also make a list of locations you would like to see on the tape. Is there a family farm? A town where the family lived for several generations? These lists will represent the ideal you should go after. Unless you have unlimited funds and can take a chunk of time off from work, you'll be accumulating your video interviews and your location shooting wherever you can, whenever you can.

Begin to gather other visuals that will aid in your interviewing. Photos and other objects of family value will help you think of questions to ask and can encourage people to talk.

PREPARING FOR THE INTERVIEW

Before you even begin to think of questions, you need to address some pertinent issues.

★ How long do you want your interviews to be? If you're talking with someone who has loads of information, you may be looking at two or three interview sessions. Don't expect someone—even a devoted relative—to sit in front of a camera and answer questions for hours on end. Limit your taping time to thirty to forty-five minutes, maximum, and certainly less if the conversation isn't flowing.

★ Ideally, where would you like the interview to take place? If you have a choice, pick a location that has some family history or that will at least enhance the conversation. A public restaurant is not the best place to do such an important taping. If you're trying to get as much as you can at a family gathering, try to set aside one room where you can have a quiet conversation.

★ Don't forget that a person who is not used to interviews and who isn't physically comfortable will not be willing to talk for long. Make sure that the seating is cozy and the area well lighted. There should be a beverage nearby, some food, and an ashtray if needed.

★ Before you begin taping, you might go through the photos, awards, or other objects that you brought, so the person will know what's coming up. The interview should not be seen as an investigative piece wherein you spring embarrassing information on your subject at an opportune time. If you're talking with an elderly person, go over the outline of your conversation ahead of time to put the person at ease.

★ If possible, have another person with you to participate in the interview. If you watch any interview programs on television, you will notice that you see both the interviewer and the person being interviewed. What you don't notice is the slew of people a few feet away, running the camera (or cameras), monitoring the audio levels, and watching the lighting.

So, if you're attempting to do everything by yourself, at least consider enlisting another family member either to run the equipment or to ask the questions. Most people are more at ease talking with another human than talking to electronic machinery. Someone sitting next to the interview subject and "discussing" the family history will most likely elicit a more natural response. However, if you can't put this together, then spend as much time as possible setting the scene with the person and encouraging stories and memories.

★ You really should use a tripod for the camera. There are people who make careers out of hand-held camerawork. They are able to give a director clearly focused and centered shots while keeping the camera balanced on a shoulder. Since you're probably not one of those individuals, you're going to get tired and crampy after five or ten minutes of holding the camera. With the camera on the tripod you can still zoom in and out on the subject, but without shouldering all the weight of the equipment.

★ Is there any way to get some physical movement into the interview? Think back to those Barbara Walters interview programs. Don't they almost always begin with a shot of Barbara and her subject walking outside or around the house? Can you do something like that with your interviewee? Can you take a tour of your subject's family home? Or at least walk over to the heirloom clock and ask how it came into the family? If the person you're interviewing doesn't get around well, maybe he will let you take a quick video tour of the house. Then, during the interview portion, you can refer back to what you saw.

★ You can also use your location footage to encourage conversation. If you have managed to swing through the town that was important to your family, mention that during an interview—"Grandma, I went through Anytown on my way to a convention last year and took some videos of the old house."

If your family still lives near a location that was important, you can always incorporate a well used interview technique—tape part of your conversation while driving through the old neighborhood. You've seen this a million times—the subject of the interview is driving a car, the camera operator is on the passenger side recording the video, and the interviewer is in the back seat. The camera operator can get shots of the interview subject, and can also record either through the windows or out the windows.

If the interview subject cannot drive, consider placing the camera operator in the back seat and the subject in the front passenger seat.

Or place both the subject and the camera operator side by side in the back seat.

CONDUCTING THE INTERVIEW

The best professional interviewers spend hours preparing for the big event. They read background materials and take notes, then organize the information into a format for the interview. In essence, they design the flow of conversation. There are certain bits of information that the interviewer knows about but wants the subject to retell in his own words. There are areas that the interviewer does not know about, and so a series of questions is designed to encourage the subject to talk about this unknown area. Despite the preparation, though, when it comes to the interview, most or even all of this preparation will vanish if the conversation takes completely unexpected turns. In such a case the good interviewer listens to what the subject is saying and jumps into the uncharted territory.

You will be a couple of steps ahead of the professional interviewer simply because you know your subject and you know a great deal about what your subject will discuss. Your first step should be to organize your material into an outline for the interview. This does not have to be overly detailed. You might just write down general areas of discussion—such as childhood, courtship and marriage, raising children, being a grandparent.

Give some thought to how you will ask your questions. Once again, fall back on your knowledge from all of the interviews you have seen on television. The best interview questions are those that require something more than just a yes or no answer.

Instead of: Did you like to dance when you were younger?
Try: What kind of music did you like to listen to?

Instead of: Did you like to read when you were a little boy?
Try: What was your favorite thing to do when you were in grade school?

This type of questioning lends itself so nicely to followup questions. A professional interviewer might have her questions plotted out, but she will try to ask the next question based on what the subject has just said. This means that the best interviewers *listen* to what is being said instead of merely thinking about the next question in their notes. An example:

Q: What kind of music did you like to listen to?
A: Well, I always liked big bands, dance music.
Q: Which bands were your favorites?
A: Hmm. Benny Goodman and Glenn Miller.
Q: Did you ever hear the bands perform live?

By doing this you will get a more conversational feel to your interview instead of a cut-and-dried question/answer/question/ answer format. The key is to listen to what's being said and ask the next question based on information just heard.

T I P

When you feel backed into a corner with your questioning, ask a why question. **"*Why* did you like the big-band sound?" "*Why* did you decide to move from Kansas to California?"**

Another method is to use *or,* to give your subject a choice to talk about. "Did you like swimming or reading better?" "Were you better at English or math?"

Some of the best questions are the most straightforward. "Can you tell me more about what it was like to live in New York City during the war?" "Why was life so hard once your family lost the farm?" We're used to television news interviews with people who probably have something to hide. Therefore, the skilled interviewer has to manipulate the questions in order to unearth the information she wants. Most of your family won't fall into the category of being on the run from the truth, and will honestly answer the questions put to them.

Remember that the photos and other props that you have

gathered can serve as springboards for questions. Ask the person to tell you about the event in the photograph, what he remembers about the people in the pictures, and why those people were important at that time. Use also the information from whatever tour you took with the camera before the video began—or use the opportunity to get some movement in the piece ("Let's go over and look at great-grand-mother's china collection now"). Or, as mentioned before, take the interview on the road.

We know that many of your interviews will not be done with much preproduction. If you're at a family reunion, you might get some photos together because you know that this will be a prime oppor-tunity for some interviews. You'll most likely be picking up those inter-views wherever you can—between meals, games, and other conver-sations. If you are at a large gathering, try to get some group interviews—a few of the siblings together, cousins, and relatives of dif-ferent generations. Seeing the family members interact and hearing them tell stories of their younger years will be great.

Here's some more help:

Sample Interview Questions for an Older Relative

Childhood and information about parents
★ Where were your parents born? What do you know about their childhoods?
★ Where did your parents meet? Courtship? What was their wedding like?
★ When were you born? Any brothers or sisters? Where did you live? Were you born at home?
★ What were your favorite activities as a child?
★ Tell us about your schooling. Were you a good student?
★ What kinds of things did your family like to do?
★ Did you have any special family traditions?

Early adulthood
★ What areas of school were you interested in?
★ What did you do once you finished school?
★ When did you move away from your parents? Why?
★ What kind of career were you interested in?

Courtship and marriage

★ How did you and your spouse meet? Tell us what the courtship was like.
★ When did you know that you were really in love?
★ How did you tell your family that you were getting married?
★ What kind of wedding did you have?

Early marriage

★ Where did you live after you were married?
★ What were your hopes for your life together?
★ What were your hopes for children? (Big family? One child?)
★ Where did the two of you go for a special outing?

Children

★ How did both of you react when you knew that a baby was on the way?
★ How did you prepare for the birth?
★ What were the pregnancy and birth like?
★ How did you feel when you brought your first baby home?
★ When did you first feel like a parent?
★ What about subsequent children? (Same questions as above.)

Being a parent

★ What was the most fun about being a parent?
★ Tell us what made you frustrated or angry.
★ Tell us what you see as the defining characteristics of your children.
★ How did you feel as your children began to grow up?
★ Did you ever think, If I knew then what I know now? If so, what word of wisdom would that be?
★ What was the most frustrating aspect of being the parent of teenagers? What was the most outrageous teenage stunt your children pulled?
★ How did it make you feel when your children began to move out and begin their adult lives?

Being a grandparent

★ Were you anxious to be a grandparent?
★ How were you told that you were going to be a grandparent? How did you feel?

★ What kinds of things did you think about during the pregnancy of your first grandchild?
★ How did you feel when the baby was born?
★ When did you first see the baby? Was it an emotional experience?
★ How easy was it for you to become a grandparent?
★ Tell us about your grandchildren. What makes each of them special to you?
★ What do you like to do best with your grandchildren?
★ What advice would you give to your own children as parents?
★ What are your hopes for your grandchildren?

Life in general
★ What kinds of things do you like to do?
★ Who are your closest friends? Why do you like them?
★ How do you think your friends would describe you?
★ Is there something that you yearn to do but haven't had a chance to do yet?
★ If you really could just do something—a fantasy, really, no cares about cost, time, or physical constraints—what would you do?
★ Is there something about you that would surprise your family if they knew of it?
★ If you could solve one (or two or three) of the country's or the world's important issues, what would it be?
★ When all is said and done, and you look around at your spouse, children, grandchildren, friends, and home, what do you think of your life?

YOUR PERSONAL VIDEO HISTORY

While you're at it, why not begin documenting the life of you and your spouse? Once again, this information is less for you than for your children. They may find it amusing to know the kind of young adult you were. You also never know what you might learn about your spouse, and vice versa.

One way to conduct this type of interview is to have the spouse who is running the camera ask the questions. Or have a close family member or friend ask them.

Sample Questions for Your Own Interview

Childhood
★ What is your earliest childhood memory?
★ How many people were in your family at the time you were born? Where did they live? What kind of work did your parents do?
★ What did you enjoy doing best as a child? What did you enjoy doing with your siblings?
★ What kind of student were you at school? What was your elementary school experience like?
★ As you went into junior high and high school, did you think you were particularly good or bad at certain subjects or sports? How did those feelings affect your outlook on school and on yourself?
★ Who were your friends in school? What kinds of things did you like to do?
★ Did you ever do anything as a teenager that you wouldn't want your own children to do?
★ What were some of the highlights of your high school years?
★ What feelings did you have about your future when you were a senior in high school?

Early Adulthood
★ Did you go to college? Why or why not?
★ If yes, can you remember your first weeks of college and what your feelings were then? When did you decide on a major, and why? Were you apprehensive about the end of college?
★ If not, what kind of job did you get after you finished high school? How did you know what kind of work you wanted to do?

Courtship and marriage
★ How did you meet? What kinds of things did you like to do on dates?
★ When did you decide that this was someone special?
★ Tell about your engagement and marriage.
★ What was your early married life like? Where did you live? What job did you have?
★ What were your hopes for your married life?
★ What were your hopes for children?

Family

★ How did you feel when you first found out that you were going to be a parent?

★ Talk a little about what being a parent means to you. What knowledge from your own parents do you want to pass on to your own children?

★ In what kind of situations do you feel confident about your parenting skills? When do you feel that you're just a kid yourself and still need help?

★ How important is your family to you?

Adulthood

★ What would your spouse be surprised to find out about you?

★ Are you comfortable with where you are in your career right now?

★ What are your main frustrations with your work, if any?

★ What makes you a good employee?

★ What kinds of hobbies do you have?

★ What aspects of family life do you enjoy most?

★ What do you like to do that brings out the child in you?

★ What to you is the most enjoyable aspect of being an adult? What's the least enjoyable aspect?

★ What would you like your children to know about you, at your age right now?

The future

★ At this point (and be sure to mark the location, date, and your age) what are your hopes for your children, for the future of your family?

★ What are your own major goals for your life? (In ten years, twenty years, what do you hope to have accomplished?)

★ It's thirty years in the future—what do you want your children to say about you? What do you want to be able to say about yourself?

What we've noticed over the years is that just about everyone we've met has a family story that's worthy of a feature film or TV miniseries. Most of us have family sagas, secrets, colorful characters, and poignant tales that could enthrall the masses. Your job is to make that miniseries or feature film with your camcorder. It may not be seen by millions, but the family members who do see it will appreciate the richness of your family history and the diversity of your family members. You'll have quite a video legacy to pass on to your children and their children.

8

ORIGINAL STORY VIDEOS: THE NEXT SPIELBERGS?

LIGHTS! CAMERA! ACTION! This is the chapter in which your family throws caution to the wind and tapes something more or less original. It's your own version of *The Swiss Family Robinson,* or *Ghostbusters,* or *Care Bears,* or all three rolled into one bizarre production. You'll look ridiculous. You'll sound incredibly silly. You'll have a lot of fun. So get ready; your script is on its way.

Once your family gets comfortable with the taping process, you should set your inhibitions aside and create your own family show. It's a chance to play together as a family; to create your own little family theatrical. This can be a great rainy day activity, or you can shoot on location in and around your home. No one need ever see the finished product except immediate family and intimate friends. However, if someone in your family happens to end up the next Steven Spielberg, undoubtedly film and video archivists will contact you for a copy of these prestigious first efforts. You never know, do you?

HOW TO START

Actors and actresses frequently use improvisation to prepare for a role, or to continue working on their acting skills. In an "improv" the players are given a small amount of information ("person walking in a snowstorm," "sad woman in a train station," "Shakespeare walking through a grocery store") and they create their character and the reasons why that person is in the situation. In essence that's what you'll be doing with your family.

If you have preschool children, follow their lead, because they're naturals at improvisation. Young children frequently make up their own stories using their favorite toys. They'll give any inanimate object a personality, they'll combine any number of plots from numerous books, films, or cartoons—and it all makes sense to them. Besides the fact that you should get some of that play acting on tape, you should also use your children's play skills as lessons for how you should approach your own original videos.

First of all, you're in it for fun. Nothing more than fun. Second, start very small; then if you're all into it, get more and more elaborate. Third, who cares if you end up with a completely unwatchable video? The camera is merely the means to get your family to do something completely out of character, pointless, and exciting.

For your first effort, you might place the camera on a tripod, locked on a wide shot of the "stage" area. If the children are putting on the play, mom or dad should hold the camera and get tighter shots of the characters and the action. If every family member is participating, the camera on a tripod will probably be the easiest way to go, although periodically one of the cast should check the shot. As your family gets more involved in these videoplays, the camera work should also become more sophisticated. Children who are old enough should be encouraged to experiment with camera movement and angles. Remember, think fun, start small, and don't be overcritical of the final video.

Okay, now you've gathered everyone around, and you're ready to begin this exercise in absurdity. Give yourself a framework that will be appropriate for your family:

★ If you have preschoolers, have the family act out a *Winnie the Pooh* story, the current favorite bedtime book, or simply assign characters ("Susan, you're Cinderella, daddy is Winnie the Pooh, mom is Raggedy Ann, and Jimmy is Baby Mickey Mouse"). If there is a story line, loosely try to follow it. Better still, let your preschoolers direct the action; they're so much more creative than adults. They can come up with all sorts of activities for an eclectic group of fantasy characters.

★ Do you have elementary age children? Why don't you all act out their current favorite film or television show, complete with some homemade costumes? Everyone should have a blast. Don't even think of assigning lines to memorize; that's not the point. Just have the kids pick out characters, decide on a story line, and go. ("We're the Ghostbusters, and we've just been called to check out this spooky house. What do you think will happen when we walk in the door?") Again, don't aim for perfection—aim for fun.

★ For older children, try a "video game" that is a variation on both improvisation and our games with the preschoolers. Put various character names on pieces of paper and then put the papers into a basket. Have everyone draw out a name. Based on the characters and their usual activities, come up with a reason why everyone might be in the same place at the same time. Act it out. Or add situations to your game and draw those out of a basket—the fun comes from trying to create a scenario that would put your Teenage Mutant Ninja Turtles at Cinderella's ball.

As your family becomes more and more adept at these videoplays, start creating characters and stories for yourself. Have your children create the character they would most like to be; you might end up with a Superhero Fairy Princess who looks like an ordinary little girl until she's called to save all of the animals in the world.

Encourage the children to begin writing down the stories before they are acted out. We're not concerned with lines and lines of dialogue, just scenes, such as:

Opening: Superboy and My Little Pony are playing by a tree in Superland. Suddenly they hear someone crying.

Scene 2: Superboy and My Little Pony find a little seal who has lost her mom and dad in a big storm.

Scene 3: Mom and dad seal are at the shore, looking for their baby seal. They decide to go into the forest to look for their baby.

Scene 4: Superboy and My Little Pony decide to take the baby seal to the sea, by going through the forest.

Scene 5: Mom and dad seal meet Superboy, My Little Pony, and their beloved baby seal. Everyone has a party.

OR

Opening: King Arthur's knights are sitting at the round table when a messenger rushes in and says that a fierce dragon has destroyed a nearby castle and taken everyone prisoner. The small kingdom needs help.

Scene 1: The knights rally their forces and discuss their plans for capturing the dragon.

Scene 2: We see the prisoners of the small kingdom at the mercy of the evil dragon. Some of the people are planning an escape.

Scene 3: Armed with a Magic Potion to splash on the dragon, the brave knights journey to the kingdom. They finally see the dragon and the prisoners.

Scene 4: Before the knights can use their Magic Potion, the dragon uses its magic powers to cast a spell on the knights and take them prisoners too.

Scene 5: Now all the prisoners attempt an escape. Will they make it? Will the Magic Potion work? Will the dragon be captured so that its powers can be used for goodness and truth? It's pandemonium as the dragon casts another spell, making everything move in slow motion. A small child is able to get close to the dragon and splash the Magic Potion on it.

Scene 6: The dragon lies in a deep sleep as the knights and people celebrate. Suddenly the dragon begins to move. People stand back, frightened. The Magic Potion has broken the spell that was on the dragon. We now see that the dragon was merely a king (or queen) who had been in a fight with an evil wizard. The king (or queen) vows to find the evil wizard and force him to do good deeds. The knights and the other people say they'll come too.

Scene 7: All ride off to find the evil wizard.

Another idea is a variation on the previous one—pulling ideas out of a basket. Have all family members write up a scene of no more than three sentences. Smaller children who can't write can dictate their scenes to a parent or older sibling. You may assemble the scenes randomly, or by age of the children, or alphabetically, using everyone's first name. However you put your scenes together, this will be your videoplay. Sure, the flow between scenes will be a little rocky, but who cares? The person who wrote a scene will serve as director for that segment and will tell the characters what to do.

Okay, okay, so it's not great literature, but you're prompting your children to write and to think creatively with a good visual sense. You're giving them good lessons in cooperation and teamwork. Plus, you're allowing each family member to be in control for a while—imagine how much fun it will be for the little ones to be able to tell their older siblings and their parents what to do and how they want them to act. We'd also suggest saving these family scripts. It will be fun to see how your children develop into storytellers.

You can use this videoplay technique to put on your own holiday plays. A Purim play, a story of the Pilgrims, or a Nativity play might be great fun. Put some planning into it and also come up with simple costumes. Painted cardboard will make great homemade set pieces. For the play itself, plan your camera work. Write an outline of the play; that will help you determine where to use a tripod and when hand-held work will look better. Remember, if you're recording your play and something goes terribly "wrong," just rewind the tape and record over it. Again, don't be hypercritical of the end result. The idea here is to have fun.

If writing a script is an accepted part of your family's videoplay, you might want to go one step further with your video techniques. Try making storyboards for your next videoplay. Storyboards are part of the preproduction of a film or television show. They allow professional directors and their production teams to visualize on paper what they want to see on screen. Most directors will storyboard virtually every shot of their film or television program. Along with writing down your ideas in script form, the storyboards will help you anticipate problem areas in your production. You might have an idea of how you would like a scene to be shot, but once you try to draw the shot it becomes clear that your idea just won't work.

The storyboarding technique is not for your first family plays. If you want to tape more complex stories and use more sophisticated

Ghostbuster meets family in trouble who needs her help.

Ghostbuster pulls door open to reveal......

Medium shot   Closeup

"Eeeeek" a ghost in the dark room!!

"Run for your lives!!!"

taping techniques, begin to incorporate storyboards into your own preproduction. A bit of advice: If you have a child who is devoted to working out scripts and storyboards, we'd advise you to get some books on film and television techniques, some biographies of great directors—and start saving for film school.

We believe these original videoplays have great potential for family fun. Once your own family is hooked, try taping a videoplay at your next birthday party or family reunion. Encourage neighborhood interaction by involving other families in your productions. It's just a way to get people to relax, to be less inhibited, to be creative—and to play.

Part III
SPECIAL
OCCASIONS

NOW WE COME TO THE BIGGIES—birthdays, vacations, Christmas, family reunions, bar and bat mitzvahs, holiday programs, children's sporting events—the reasons that most of us bought our video equipment in the first place. These occasions represent important milestones for any family and just beg to be immortalized on film or tape. But before you jump in and start taping, you'll be well served to take a few of our special-occasion lessons. Otherwise, like the rest of us, you'll have some major *faux pas* committed to videotape for all future generations to see. Wouldn't you rather have your grandchildren say, "What a wonderful Christmas that must have been!" instead of, "Gee, Gramps never quite got the hang of that old camcorder, did he?" Well, to assure yourself that you'll never end up like Gramps, read on.

Whenever you pull out your camcorder for any special occasion, you're probably counting on capturing the heart and soul of that event. All too often, though, you may miss those nuances and end up with a video that has nothing of the life and fun that were there. Part of the "blame" for this comes from the fact that it's very rare to make a video that's as special as the event itself. The rest of the blame may be on you because of your shooting style. Maybe in your zeal to get things on tape you neglected that very important responsibility of actively participating in the occasion. Your children may feel hurt because they see you spending more time with your camcorder than with them. Or your spouse may feel slightly put upon because she ended up coordinating the event while you had the fun of floating around and shooting videos.

We've mentioned this before but it's doubly important whenever you're part of a special occasion. Every time you pick up your camcorder you need to ask yourself—Am I maintaining a good balance between documenting and participating in this event?

A simple thought? Surely, but it's one that's crucial for you to remember. We firmly believe that when it comes to special occasions it's the occasion that's special. Getting it all down on tape is important, but it's even more important to remember—if there's no fun family event taking place, there surely won't be any fun family video.

Keeping a balance between documenting and participating is of the utmost importance. Your home videos should always supplement the occasion and not override it. Too much video and you take the chance of killing the soul of the occasion. Too little video and you risk missing out on capturing something that you'd want to remember forever. A balance between the two is what you're after and if you have to lean one way or the other, let it be on the side of participating. It will always be better to have slightly shorter videos of a fun family event than full-length documentaries of a disgruntled family perpetually missing one member.

9
BIRTHDAYS

O AHEAD, name an occasion that's more suited for a camcorder than a birthday party. Birthdays, especially children's, have a magic to them that seems to capture the essence of that year in a child's life. A good birthday party video is something everyone will want to view again and again; whereas a bad birthday video will very likely become an embarrassment. And what, you ask, makes the difference between a good video and a bad one? Planning. When you take the time before the party to sit down and decide who will be responsible for each area—that's the kind of planning that will help make a great party.

Besides the easy decisions on decorations and the flavor of the cake, there are several other areas that will require some serious consideration. Two of the most important areas are: planning a shooting schedule and handing out the party assignments.

PLANNING A SHOOTING SCHEDULE

Make a rough shooting script for yourself. Think about which parts of the party you'll want to shoot and how much time you want to devote to each. Remember, you want to tell a complete video story, with a beginning, a middle, and an end.

HANDING OUT PARTY ASSIGNMENTS

Decide ahead of time who will be handling each chore. It always helps to have some assistance with the party and even two or three helpers isn't too many. With extra helpers you can assign party areas and decide who will handle each chore. Some separate party assignments might be:

★ Answering the door.
★ Organizing the games or the entertainment.
★ Serving the food and drinks.
★ Cleaning up.
★ Lighting the candles and carrying in the cake.
★ Cutting and serving the cake.
★ Carrying in the presents and keeping track of who sent each.
★ Handing out the party favors.
★ Helping the guests gather up their things when it's time to go.

T I P

When you divide up the party assignments, make sure that using the camcorder is also included. Everyone should see at least a little of himself on videotape. It's not a party video unless there is footage of everyone.

These all may seem like picky details but organizing job assignments is crucial for a well run party. When you and your helpers have specific areas to concentrate on, you'll have the freedom of knowing just when you can concentrate on recording and when you'll need to help with the party. In the best of all possible worlds you would probably have enough extra helpers to take care of the work part of the party leaving you to enjoy the event and record whenever you like.

Don't forget that your trusty tripod can be a great help during the party. In Chapter 5 we told you how one parent and a camcorder on a tripod could tape a child's birthday party. So even if you've got other people to help you, a camera on a tripod can let you both tape and enjoy the event. Someone should be assigned to the camcorder-tripod to make sure that the location is changed periodically and that the camera records for no more than five minutes at a time.

T I P

We don't know whether this is a tip or a warning. If you're using a tripod on a locked-off shot during your child's party, remember that a child's height is about the same as that of an adult's rear end. We're serious about this. We saw on video a whole birthday party of delightful children . . . and adult posteriors. Remember, learn from the mistakes of others. Check your tripod shot before you begin recording. For heaven's sake, remember where the camera is and don't stand in front of it.

Keep in mind, you're after highlights of the birthday party, not a minute-by-minute account of the entire thing. We've seen birthday videos that ran for an hour and bred more boredom than enjoyment. Friends of ours have videos (we've seen them) made by someone they hired to record their child's entire party. And that's what they got. Over an hour of videotape containing shots and conversations of all the parents there and more footage of the party than they can ever use. The person who recorded the party assumed that our friends would edit the footage into a more viewable length. Unfortunately, they never got around to it and now they've got a v-e-r-y long birthday video.

So, unless you are planning to edit all your footage, keep your tape brief. Fifteen minutes are usually sufficient for any birthday party, so keep this limit in mind as you're recording. Keep thinking highlights and record only a sample of each event.

The main focus of the birthday party day is the birthday child and the birthday celebration—the cake, candles, and singing; not the opening of each present or the playing of each game in its entirety. With some extra help and a little bit of organization you'll be able to devote more time to videotaping without having to worry about wrangling kids or cleaning up messes.

Every child waits all year for this one day so you should make it extra special. To give you some video ideas, we've broken down a typical birthday party into a shooting script that has worked for us.

A HAPPY BIRTHDAY VIDEO

Getting Ready for the Party

A wonderful way to start off your birthday video is to record some of the preparations for the party. With younger children the anticipation is nearly as enjoyable as the party itself, so use your camcorder to help add to the excitement. Some of the preparty activities you should look for are:

★ filling the goody bags
★ making and decorating the cake
★ getting the party decorations ready and hung
★ picking out the birthday party clothes

Preparty Interview

On the day of the birthday party itself take a couple of minutes and do a little interview with the birthday child. Ask questions like:

★ Are you excited?
★ What do you think will be the best part of the day?
★ What kind of presents are you hoping for?
★ Did you help with the cake? How many candles are on it?

You get the idea. Keep trying to build up your child's excitement for that big event to come.

The Arrival of the Guests

A cute way to start the actual party is to shoot a little video of each guest arriving. A couple of seconds of each child will suffice (include a voice-over that mentions names). Record as many arrivals as you can, but don't feel bad if you miss a couple. What you're after is some video showing that the guests are here and the party is starting.

Entertainment

Entertainment and games can make or break any child's party. Unfortunately, it's a fact of childhood that the mark of a successful party is enjoyable entertainment. This is an area where your preparty organization will be put to the test. If you feel that this will require all of your attention, focus on the entertainment first, then try to shoot some video. If party games are to be the only entertainment, record a bit of one or two—just something to convey the feeling that games were played and that everybody had a great time playing them.

If your party is to have a professional entertainer present, use the same strategy. But it's crucial for you to remember: don't get carried away. All you want on tape is a sample of the performance, not the entire thing. You'll never want to watch a complete twenty-minute puppet show or fifteen minutes of a costumed character talking to each birthday guest. Keep your coverage short and keep thinking highlights.

That Moment of Moments—
The Presentation of the Birthday Cake

You had better be ready when this takes place or you will have a birthday party video without the birthday. So don't forget this tip: Double-check your batteries and tape a few minutes before cake time. Then, set yourself up in a spot where you'll be able to see the birthday cake enter the room and be able to follow it all the way to the birthday child. The very best angle will allow you to see both your child's face

The perfect camera angle allows you to see both action and faces at the same time.

and the lighted candles. Start rolling tape before the cake enters the room and keep rolling all through "Happy Birthday" and the blowing out of the candles. This is the biggest moment of the entire party so it's definitely not a time to be stingy with videotape.

Opening the Gifts

More and more families are adopting the custom of opening the birthday presents after all the guests have gone home. Doing this eliminates many of the hurt feelings or embarrassment resulting from duplicate gifts or receiving toys that the child already has. Whether you decide to open the gifts during the party or after, your video coverage will be essentially the same.

Again, this is an occasion in which you will want to see both your child's face and what she is doing. Be sure to keep thinking highlights and videotape only a couple of gifts being opened. If you're to send your finished video to distant relatives, and they've sent gifts, make it a point to tape the opening of those presents. Of course, you'll be taking the chance that your child's response to Aunt Edna's hand-picked gift may embarrass her. But that's part of the fun of videotaping. Besides, if her reaction is too "honest," you can always stop, back up the tape, and record over it. Honesty may *not* always be the best policy.

Postparty Interview

Since you have done a little preparty interview, why not wrap up things with a postparty interview after all the excitement has died down? If it's been a great party, you'll have one tired kid and that will say a lot by itself. Quietly ask some simple questions:

★ Was it a great party?
★ What was the best part?
★ Tell us about your favorite gift.
★ What will next year's party be like?

T I P

Consider using just one tape to record a child's consecutive birthday parties. Four or five birthdays in a row can give you a real sense of the uniqueness of your child. Keep each year's coverage tight and around ten to fifteen minutes long.

OR

If you're really good at using your camcorder, you may be able to add to the party through your interaction with the children. Be an interviewer or play hide and seek (with you and the camcorder doing the seeking). Anything you can do that keeps them happy and energetic will be worth its weight in gold on videotape.

10
VACATIONS

SK TEN PEOPLE this question, "What's your favorite thing to record with your camcorder?" and at least half will answer vacations. For some reason most of the world seems to feel that camcorders and vacations go together like peanut butter and jelly. Unfortunately, sending most of us on vacation with a camcorder is a lot like sending our kids into the kitchen to make peanut butter and jelly sandwiches. We end up with something, but it doesn't look quite as it's supposed to.

So, how come? If camcorders and vacations are the perfect match, why don't the results show it? Our guess is that most people don't quite know how to go about shooting a vacation video. They have some basics down but the rest of the coverage seems to fall short. If your vacation videos tend to look like our PB & J example, maybe you should ask yourself these vacation video questions.

1. Why do I go on a vacation anyway?
A. To relax.
B. To escape everyday worries and get away from it all.

C. To shoot vacation videos.

2. Why do I shoot videos of my vacation?
A. Because that's what one is supposed to do on a vacation.
B. To remember what my vacation was like.
C. Because it's fun and everybody enjoys watching the tapes over and over again.

If your answer to question 1 was C, you *do* need a vacation. We believe that A and B are much more appropriate answers. After all, if you spend too much of your time making videos, you're still working, and not vacationing.

As for question 2, B and C are the better answers. If you find yourself leaning toward answer A, watch out. You're letting yourself get sucked into the vacation video hype. Vacations are supposed to be for fun and relaxation, not for shooting two hours of videotape a day.

So, you ask, How can I make great vacation videos? Well, you've asked the right question. After we're through with this section you'll be champing at the bit to go on vacation again. There are a couple of tricks to remember but mostly we will lead you through a few commonsense tips that you probably know but aren't applying to your vacations.

The simplest tip is an idea that keeps popping up again and again. Even when you're on vacation you must strike a balance between documenting and participating. Otherwise you won't have a vacation worth documenting. Don't get carried away with your camcorder. You're taking a vacation to relax and the best vacation videos serve only to help you remember how relaxed you were. What you shoot with your camcorder is supposed to enhance the memory of your vacation, not be a substitute. Don't end up living the old joke, "Hurry up, kids; we'll enjoy the view when we get home."

One video "trick" that seems always to work is to use your camcorder to liven up your vacation. Vacations mean fun and there are many ways to capture that fun on tape. The very best way is to make your videos personal and involve the entire family. Do some interviews, fool around, be goofy. If your videos border on being embarrassing, you're probably doing a good job.

HOW TO SHOOT FUN VACATION VIDEOS

Think About It Ahead of Time

A little bit of planning goes a long way, especially if you will be traveling. All we're asking you to do is to think about your vacation before you leave. Take a few minutes to make a short list of things you think might look nice on video. Don't drive yourself crazy. You're not producing an actual shooting script. We merely want you to get into the frame of mind of thinking about your vacation videos. Maybe a couple of nice things—scenic vistas from the mountains, fishing in a meltwater stream, roasting marshmallows over the campfire.

What this thinking will lead to is the daily outline you should put together once you're on vacation. Every morning, maybe over breakfast, take a few moments to think about that day's events and come up with a plan for putting them on tape. If you're going hiking that day, think of a quick introduction that will set the stage for everything to come. Half a minute is all it takes. If your introduction seems corny, so much the better. Corny intros are fun and if your tape starts with fun, the rest of the day will follow suit. Don't drive yourself crazy either. Just because you're pondering the day's events doesn't mean that spontaneity is tossed out the window. All you need to do is set up a frame of mind for shooting videos. The spontaneity that will flow during the rest of the day is what will make your vacation videos special.

Think Highlights

Remember those vacation home movies you grew up with? Don't fall into the same trap. All you, or anybody else, will ever want to watch is a sampler of each day's events. You won't have any friends left if you subject them to five hours of video every time you return from vacation. Think highlights and don't worry if you decide to skip a day here and there. All a good vacation video can ever hope to be is a recap of how nice your vacation was. If people wanted to see five hours of your vacation, they would have gone along with you.

Of course, a few occasions will demand longer video pieces. Because we keep stressing highlights doesn't mean that every event must have the same amount of coverage. You don't need a video calendar of every single day. But, when something big does come along, be sure to cover it in detail. Side trips are what make a vacation a vacation. Skip a day of shooting if you want to, but when it's time for something fun, shoot a quick introduction and go.

Think about shooting a couple of mood pieces too. You can capture the feel of a vacation by shooting a couple of static or slow pan shots with no other sound than the natural sound that's present. To get the most out of this idea look for a shot that captures the feeling of your location. Perhaps a slow fifteen-second pan showing the timeless view from a mountain lookout or maybe one or two minutes of an icy mountain stream rushing by the camera. This type of shot can work anywhere, from the beach to a hotel balcony in the middle of a city. Wherever you choose to shoot a mood piece, you'll be taken back to that spot every time you watch that tape. Five or ten years from now you will close your eyes and remember exactly what it was like to be right there. That's what a vacation video is for.

Think Fun

When you think about it, aren't the best videos about the things you don't get to see or experience every day? If your vacation is helping you to escape your everyday life, keep an eye open for the sights that are different. If you're traveling, shoot some video of the different-looking cars, houses, streets, and stores. Grab a quick shot of a newspaper vendor or a roadside restaurant. Look for closeups of people's faces or even some shots of the local newspapers, television, or radio. (Remember, if you wish to take a stranger's photograph or video, be polite—ask for permission first.) If you're in a foreign country, this may be the only occasion you'll have to visit there. Shooting lots of video bits of simple, everyday things will help you capture the memories of a lifetime.

Don't be afraid to be adventuresome with your camcorder. In video, the unusual can be fun. Look for camera angles that are different from the same old shoulder-height shots you've been shooting. Try shooting from ground level or from over your head. Or how about starting a shot angled to one side and then straightening it up as you pan to something else?

Another way to personalize your vacation videos even more is to make them humorous. Some of the funniest videos we've seen showed family members offering satiric on-camera comments about what we had just seen. "Just how do you really feel?" asked one who had been through Disney World's A Small World ride for the umpteenth time. This style of shooting works best with teenagers or adults, but you can also adapt it to small children.

What can be cute is to have your child act as a commentator for what you're shooting at that moment. Have her describe the ride you're on or comment on why she doesn't want to ride the upside down roller coaster. The spontaneous comments from your kids are a surefire means to a funny vacation video.

A FUN VACATION VIDEO

One point you should always keep in mind: your vacation video should tell a story. Think beginning, middle, and end to your video.

VACATION TRIP TO THE MOUNTAINS

Introduction to This Year's Trip

Be sure to shoot some of the prevacation events. Start with a map unfolding, then show a finger pointing to your destination. While you're shooting this include a voice-over announcing the name of the place and what year this is. Shoot some of the packing and the loading of the car.

Traveling to the Mountains

Record some scenery through the windshield as you're driving along the road. Naturally, this should be done by a passenger and not the driver. You don't want your vacation to end before it starts. Get a shot or two of the people inside the car or at a rest stop—something that conveys the feeling of traveling to your destination.

Arrival at the Mountains

This is the time to look for a scenic vista shot or to elicit a couple of comments from the family on how the day has been. If the stress level isn't too high, try recording a bit of the search for a campsite or the cabin. Then, if things are still going well, some of the unloading of the car and the settling in.

If the day is nearly over, think of something to wrap up the first day's video. Something that shows you're glad to be there. Maybe a quiet shot of some tired children or a short comment by an adult.

First Real Day of Vacation

If any day needs an introduction, this is it. Something to set the tone for the rest of the vacation. How about a closeup shot of a smug dad saying, "I'm on vacation, I'm happy, and I'm going to have a great time." While you're at it, have dad mention what the day's events will be.

Whenever you take your camcorder with you, it's important to introduce each piece that is about to be shot. If you're setting off on a hike, do a voice-over with a pretty shot and say something like, "We're going to start off with a five-mile hike and this is the beginning of the trail." Follow up any videos you shot during the hike with some video of your lunch break and the trip back to camp.

Then forget about videos for the rest of the day unless you find something funny that shows how tired everybody is after the morning outing. Recap your day around the campfire. Try to capture a little of the feeling of being there—a song, some jokes, that sort of thing.

Days 2, 3, 4 . . .

Continue shooting videos of your vacation following the format we've discussed. Skip a day, skip an event, but always try to capture the highlights of your vacation. Remember, you're telling a story and every story needs a beginning, middle, and end.

VACATION VIDEO PREPARATION TIPS

If you're going to go through the effort of planning for your vacation, take some extra time to check out your video equipment too. It is wise to do this one or two weeks ahead of time because if you find anything wrong, you'll still have enough time to get it fixed. Even if you feel that your equipment is working fine, set aside a half hour and examine it anyway. Better to find a problem now than later.

Equipment Checklist

BATTERIES:
Have at least two batteries if not three. Each should be individually marked with a number or letter. Test to see that each holds a full charge.

BATTERY CHARGER:
Test your charger to be sure it works correctly.

TAPES:
Pack one or two new tapes, enough to provide you with one extra hour of recording time. Keep them in your camera case so they won't get misplaced.

CABLES AND ADAPTORS:
Check that you have the appropriate cables to connect your camcorder to any television set. Be sure you have the correct adaptors too.

CAMCORDER:
Check that your camcorder is in proper working order. Make a test recording, then play it back. Look for static or a noisy picture, anything that might indicate that your camcorder isn't working as well as it should. Make sure that the lens and viewfinder are free from dust and smudges.

Of course, not all vacations will take place during sunny seventy-five-degree weather. Sometimes you may run into conditions less than ideal for recording videos. But even if it's raining or 110 in the shade, you don't have to stop using your camcorder. A little common sense and a couple of our camcorder tips can keep you going no matter what the conditions.

❖❖❖❖❖❖❖❖❖❖❖❖❖❖❖❖❖❖❖❖❖❖❖❖❖❖❖❖❖❖

T I P 1
Keep Your Camcorder Comfortable

Make it a point never to leave your camcorder directly exposed to the sun. The most common culprit is the interior of your car where on a hot, sunny day it can reach 140 degrees — in the shade. If you must leave video equipment in the car, shade it from the sun's direct rays with a coat or piece of cloth. But, please, leave an air gap between the covering and the equipment. If there isn't a gap, all you're doing is aiding the baking process. It's the air space that helps lessen the temperature. Ten or fifteen degrees may be the difference between safety and a cooked camcorder. Always keep your equipment comfortable and you'll be happier for it.

❖❖❖❖❖❖❖❖❖❖❖❖❖❖❖❖❖❖❖❖❖❖❖❖❖❖❖❖❖❖

T I P 2
Make a Raincoat for Your Camcorder

Everyone knows you shouldn't let your camcorder get wet. It cost you a bundle to begin with, and will cost you time and (perhaps) patience in trying to dry it out. You can, however, use your camcorder when it's raining *if* you take certain precautions.

Several manufacturers make clear plastic rain covers which will allow you to operate your camcorder in even the wettest conditions. These covers usually have clear glass windows for the lens and viewfinder plus an opening at the bottom of the cover for your hand. Their only drawback is they cost more than most of us are willing to spend. What you can do, though, is make your own rain cover based on the same design.

(1) Take a plastic bag that will fit over your camcorder and place it over the camera so that the opening is at the bottom. Make sure the bag is large enough to include your hand that operates the controls. (2) Now, cut one

small hole in the front of the bag just large enough for the lens to poke through, then cut another small hole in the back so you can see the viewfinder. (3) Take a small piece of tape and wrap it around the plastic bag at the viewfinder hole so the viewfinder doesn't poke out and get wet. That's it. Now you have a rain cover and you're ready to shoot.

This plastic cover will keep your camcorder dry enough to shoot in light rain. The only thing you need to keep an eye on is the two openings for the lens and view-finder. Don't allow *any* water to run down either opening by letting the plastic bag pull away. Only the very ends of the lens and viewfinder should be exposed. Secondly, if you have a hat, wear it. The bill of the hat will offer a bit more protection, especially for the viewfinder.

This trick can let you keep taping under most vacation conditions. But, if you want to make a habit of taping in the rain, spend the money and invest in a professional rain cover. It is specially made for wet conditions and the protection it offers is much more reassuring than anything you can rig up.

Accessories to Consider Bringing

★ A tripod or monopod
★ Lens brush and lens paper for cleaning
★ Plastic bag for use as a rain cover
★ Marking pen and 3″ × 5″ cards for making titles
★ Electrical adaptors for battery charger (if you're traveling in a foreign country)
★ A small, comfortable carry bag for your camcorder and extra supplies (it's easier to use than your full-size traveling case)

That's it. If everything has been checked out and is ready to go, so are you. Vacation videos are fun and easy to make, especially when you're prepared and confident that everything will work. Enjoy your vacation, but don't forget:

Think highlights and think about making your vacation fun.

11
CHRISTMAS
AND HANUKKAH

HEN YOU THINK ABOUT
Christmas and Hanukkah what kind of images come to mind? Do you picture choirs singing Christmas carols in peaceful evening church services? Lighted Menorahs against frosty windows? Selecting your Christmas tree from the corner lot, then carting it home to be decorated? Platters of savory potato *latkes*? The scent of cookies baking in the oven? The sounds of wrapping paper and tape?

Whatever the image, you're thinking about family and traditions. Christmas and Hanukkah are perfectly suited to making a great video that your family will actually want to watch. Your biggest challenge will be, again, balancing the documenting and participating aspects. We have some ideas to help you meet that challenge *and* end up with a memorable tape for your family's video library.

CHRISTMAS

Christmas is one of those times when the day itself is more important than any home video. It is a special occasion which home videos should capture through highlights, not with several hours of nonstop taping. If your entire Christmas morning is on videotape, then someone in your family missed participating in this important family holiday. Christmas morning is hectic enough as it is without adding a major videotape production.

We have a few ideas that will help you get some of that Christmas Day on tape without devoting a huge chunk of time to it. Most of the ideas are simple and all of them will contribute to capturing the family feeling that's so much a part of this day.

Getting Ready

One key to making your camcorder an unobtrusive part of the occasion is to have everything ready ahead of time. All your equipment should be pulled out, loaded, charged, and ready. If you have a tripod or plan to use auxiliary lights, pull them out too. Come Christmas morning you will need to do no more than turn on your camcorder, switch on a light, and shoot.

Another key is to tape the opening for your Christmas video ahead of time. All you need is an introduction, like a shot of your children's note to Santa or anything else that says Christmas—maybe a pretty shot of the lighted tree or a slow pan shot of all the cards displayed on the mantle. Go ahead. Come up with something. This is your chance to be artistic.

To start off on the right foot, remember that Christmas involves the whole family. Your videotape should have pieces of everybody interacting, opening gifts, picking up trash, whatever. None of this dad-shooting-all-the-videos stuff. Pass the camera around (and please remember to stop recording while passing it).

Below are some ideas we've come across that will help you capture the feeling of Christmas with your camcorder. The more of them that you incorporate into your video, the better it will be.

★ Create the look and mood of Christmas

Music: Have Christmas music playing in the background. Not only will it sound pretty on your tape; it will make your day feel more Christmassy.

Lights: Make sure the Christmas tree lights are turned on. If you have a fireplace or any decorative candles, think about lighting them to give the room a warm, cozy feel.

★ Try to make everybody look good

If your house celebrates by opening gifts on Christmas morning, consider opening a few presents and then taking a break. After you have eaten breakfast and dressed, then you can go back to opening gifts and shooting more videos. Since you are to be immortalized on tape, you might as well look your best.

★ Make sure everybody is on tape

Every adult and older child should have an opportunity to use the camcorder. It's also fun to set the camera on a tripod and shoot a wide shot of everyone. Just pick a good spot in the room from which everyone's face can be seen, then roll tape. Shoot only a couple of minutes of this though. Five minutes should be the maximum from any one location. If you want to shoot more, change the camera angle and limit each additional shot to two minutes.

★ Capturing the kids on tape

If your children are opening presents and playing on the floor, get down there with them. Don't shoot everything from your height; shoot some video from their level too. A good video has plenty of closeups and Christmas is full of great opportunities for special shots. During the opening of gifts, look for intent faces and the reactions of those watching. Don't forget to shoot some quick videos of boxes being opened, toys being played with, and your children amid piles of wrapping paper and mountains of trash.

★ Remember, think highlights

What you want from the day is a video that captures the feeling of what your Christmas was like. You don't need to include every gift being opened and every toy being played with. Remember, this is a family day. If you get too carried away with your camcorder you may end up with a video filled with tense and angry people. Participate and enjoy. Merry Christmas!

A MERRY CHRISTMAS VIDEO

Remember two key rules: Give your tape a beginning, middle, and end. Second, check your equipment and set it up ahead of time.

Christmas Eve Introduction

With seasonal music in the background, open your tape with a closeup shot of your decorated and lighted Christmas tree. Voice-over the intro:

CAMERA OPERATOR: Merry Christmas! It's Christmas Eve and there's nothing left to do except wait for Santa.

or

CHILDREN: It's Christmas. We've got cookies and milk ready for Santa. We've got presents.

or a combination

CAMERA OPERATOR: Why are you kids so excited?
CHILDREN: It's Christmas Eve.
CAMERA OPERATOR: What happens tonight?
CHILDREN: Santa comes! . . .

Record some montage shots of your home at Christmas (seven to ten seconds, maximum, for each shot) with voice-over of what we're seeing, and why ("This is the nativity scene that Jenny made in Scouts this year"):

★ Christmas wreath
★ decorated mantel
★ nativity scene
★ children's Christmas artwork
★ Christmas card display

Preparing for Christmas Morning

Once parental duties are out of the way, set up your tripod and auxiliary light, if you plan to use them. Be sure to check your tape supply and batteries. In fact, have some batteries charging so that they'll be ready by morning.

Think how you expect the morning to begin and then plan where to keep the camera.

★ Do the kids usually run into the parents' room? If so, keep the camera there.
★ Does the whole event begin at treeside? Put the camera there so someone can grab it easily.

Plan the beginning of the day. One spouse should grab the camera and turn on the auxiliary light; the other should turn on the tree lights and put on some music.

Christmas Morning

Now the excitement begins. Perhaps like this: The children have run into the room with tree and presents. The parents have followed at a fast pace—amazing really, for still being half asleep—and have completed their tasks. Lights are on, music plays softly in the background, children are already bouncing off the walls, and someone is holding the video camera. First shot is a wide, panning shot of the Christmas room. Voice-over: "Merry Christmas! It's Christmas morning."

Next, try to get around to all the family members. Record some medium to closeup shots, and get initial reactions to the bounty from Santa. Don't try to walk with the camera recording. It's easier, faster, and looks better to record a reaction, stop tape, move to another person, and begin recording again. Ask questions:

★ How did all these presents get here?
★ Do you think one of these presents might be for you?
★ How does this special morning make you feel?

Take a break and stop recording. It's probably time to help the little ones find a gift to open—or corral the older children from ripping into everyone else's gifts. Take some time to get your family organized and started on their Christmas morning ritual. For mom and dad this might mean taking that morning shower and grabbing a cup of coffee.

The Morning Continues

With the camcorder on a tripod, begin recording the distribution of gifts and the unwrapping. Plan to leave the tripod in one position for maybe five minutes. Although time goes quickly on this morning, watching ten or fifteen minutes of a static camera shot will not be interesting. Follow a loose schedule:

★ Tape for five minutes or for two or three gifts
★ Stop taping for ten to fifteen minutes
★ Change tripod position
★ Tape for five minutes
★ Stop taping for ten to fifteen minutes
★ Change tripod position
★ Etc.

Once the morning is under way and the kids are absorbed with the unwrapping and playing, take the camera off the tripod and let it interact with the children from time to time.

★ Is your daughter playing with a new doll set? Get down with her and ask about the new present. Does the doll have a name? Who was it from? Does your daughter have a special message for the person who gave the gift?
★ Using a wide shot, pan around the room and record the presents, wrapping paper, children playing with toys, older family members talking and unwrapping gifts.
★ Get some comments from the adults. Do mom or dad have any comments about Christmas morning?
★ When the presents are all unwrapped, slowly pan the roomful of boxes and wrapping paper, and have the entire family say, "Merry Christmas!"

The Rest of the Day and Mealtime

Periodically throughout the day, grab the camcorder and record the activities of family members. You'll want to show the children, bundled up and playing outside with new sleds. Or if you live in warmer climates, riding new bikes or playing with new sports equipment.

If your family prepares a big Christmas meal, head for the kitchen and walk through some of the preparations. Get some shots of the food cooking on the stove. Ask the cook about particular recipes being used (any family significance?). And make certain someone recites the menu for the upcoming meal.

As mealtime nears, move the tripod to a location that will give you a nice wide shot of the meal area. Try to scope out at least one more area too, so you can have at least two angles from which to tape. Remember, think highlights. You don't need the entire meal in real time.

Tape the beginning of the meal—once everyone has been seated (or as people are called to a buffet table)—especially if there is a family prayer. Apply a five-minute time limit to your taping, unless there is an unusually memorable conversation going on (maybe some funny family stories) or something else worth keeping on tape. Now comes the part you've been waiting for—stop tape and enjoy the meal. About two-thirds of the way through the meal, get up and move the tripod and camera to your second taping area and tape for another five minutes.

If there is a children's table, it might be fun to take the camera over and ask how things are going. Questions like:

★ How's the food?
★ What don't you like?
★ What tastes best?
★ What do you think Santa has for Christmas dinner?

Get an end-of-the-meal signoff around dessert time. Ask the group what the favorite dessert was, ask for a round of applause for all the cooks who prepared the meal, and ask a family member for some final words of thanks for such a great dinner.

End of the Day

Once again, make sure the tree lights are on and music is playing. Begin with a closeup of the tree. Zoom out to show family members gathered around, full from a great meal and tired from an exciting day.

★ Ask everyone what this Christmas meant to them.
★ Ask the children what their favorite part of the day was.

★ Ask what feelings family members have as the day draws to a close.

★ As you pan over and end with a final shot of the lighted tree, have your children, or the entire family, say, "Merry Christmas!"

Every family has its own holiday traditions. Injected into anyone's Christmas video should be the little elements that make your family's Christmas special. A family we know has a tradition of going room to room in their house, all members holding hands while the person in front rings a bell. One year the parents recorded this event by simply setting the camera on a tripod. It helped that their home was on one level, but you heard the bell ringing, the running, and the laughter throughout the short tape piece, and you saw the family running across the camera shot one way, then back again another way, then not at all for a second or two, then back into the main room. Although not a polished professional job, the recording captured a tradition that meant much to their family. It looked fun too.

HANUKKAH

Like Christmas, Hanukkah is a festive family holiday that has many variations within a set structure. That structure is a candlelighting ceremony every evening for eight consecutive evenings. Some families make each night a celebration with gift giving. Other families will observe the candlelighting for seven nights and have their big cele-

You can use an auxiliary light bounced off the wall to increase the base light level while not overwhelming the candlelight from the Menorah.

bration on the final night. Still other families may use the Hanukkah season as an excuse for a nice big holiday party. Whatever your observance, you should try to tape the ritual of Hanukkah as a keepsake for your family.

At the very least, one year plan to tape the candlelighting ceremony. Since this takes place in the evening, you'll probably need an auxiliary light. This light can be positioned so that it will give added base light but not detract from the lights of the candles. Of course, if you'd like a more natural effect, and your camera can tolerate low-light levels, you can tape using available light. This effect would very likely enhance the solemnity of the prayers.

Getting Ready

Take time beforehand to try a couple of shot tests:

★ Does your family traditionally hold the candlelighting ceremony in the same place? Take out your camcorder and see what the shots will look like. Maybe you can position people in certain areas so as to get both candles and people in the same picture.
★ Is your family's ceremony movable? Look for a few areas in your home that might look nice. Again, ideally you'd like to see people and the Menorah in the picture.

Wherever your family's ceremony may take place, figure out at least three shot variations for the tripod—for example, from the left, from the right, and from the opposite side of the Menorah (so the Menorah is in the foreground, and participants' faces can be seen).

As for lights, do some practice taping with an auxiliary light on, then with only available light, and see which you like better.

T I P

Use a separate, high-quality tape for this series of videotapes. If this is something you do not intend to do annually, you will also want to store this cassette in a special place.

The Ceremony

Remember, think beginning, middle, and end for the whole tape, not just eight individual nights. Therefore, set up an introductory piece. Examples:

★ If there is an older relative who is participating, ask him to explain what Hanukkah means, and perhaps tell about a special holiday in his life.

★ If there are lots of young children involved, have someone ask the children what they think the significance of the holiday is.

★ Remember the opening to "Masterpiece Theatre" on Public Television? Where the camera floats in and around framed photographs? Well, gather together some family photos—prop them up if they're not framed—and, with appropriate music in the background, slowly move from one photo to the next. Voice-over that this is Hanukkah and the first night's celebration is about to begin.

Set your camera on the tripod, locked off to the shot you've set up before the ceremony. Don't start recording until you are ready to begin the ceremony. Make sure the participants know where to stand so they won't block the shot.

Record the ceremony, very simply, in its entirety. The point is, let the camera observe what your family did in one particular year. After the ceremony, stop recording.

If your family gives presents each night, move your camera and tripod to the area where the gifts will be distributed. This is a time to think highlights. Remember, record for no more than five minutes, then stop tape. You don't want to end up with thirty minutes of a locked-off shot while several different conversations are going on and present-unwrapping frenzy abounds. Five minutes maximum, then either change the tripod position or take the camera off the tripod.

If you do decide to go for a hand-held look, remember to edit in the camera. As you are shooting, get closeups of people and small-group shots, and ask for some responses to gifts. But, think short shots as opposed to three to four minutes on each person or group. Review Chapter 3 to refresh your editing skills.

If your family hosts a larger party on any of the nights, take the camera and circulate amongst the activities:

★ Small-group conversations
★ Children unwrapping gifts
★ Preparation of the *latkes*
★ Table full of food (ask one of the guests to lead you on a tour of the traditional foods, or at least the special recipes brought by family and friends)

In closing this first night's ceremony, have a family member or members express their feelings about Hanukkah season and end on a shot of the Menorah, with one candle lighted.

The Second Through Eighth Night

Think beginning, middle, and end of the individual pieces. Unless your family has a traditional celebration after each night's ceremony, stop recording as soon as the candlelighting and prayers are over.

Remember to introduce each night's taping ("This is Hanukkah, the third night") and end each night's piece with a shot of the Menorah, with one more candle lighted. Try to vary the tripod shot for the ceremony each night, just for variety's sake. One night you might forgo participation for the sake of documenting and concentrate on medium shots and closeups of family members.

If there were some children with questions or thoughts about Hanukkah on the first night, you might ask, midweek, if they now understand better, or have clearer feelings about the holiday.

The Final Night

Before the ceremony, introduce the night as the final night of Hanukkah. Ask for comments from all family members about this year's holiday; about how they've felt as the week has progressed. Cover the ceremony as you have throughout the week.

Some families save their gift giving for the final night. If this is your family's night for a larger celebration, cover as outlined before. Be sure to incorporate lots of short shots, reactions of people, Hanukkah decorations, tired children, and discarded boxes, wrapping paper, and ribbons.

If there is a family matriarch or patriarch at this final night's ceremony, ask them for a comment, a wish for Hanukkah, a wish for the family. Or, ask the same of your children and your spouse. End your documentation of Hanukkah with a shot of the fully lighted Menorah.

Obviously, you should modify the schedule of your taping according to the way your family celebrates Hanukkah. Deciding to tape your Hanukkah celebration is a big commitment, but try it at least once. This is the kind of tape your family will cherish for years to come, we guarantee.

12
WEDDINGS

EDDINGS! What is it about these truly special occasions that touch a soft spot in all our hearts? Is it the sight of a loving couple prepared to embark on one of the most important journeys of their lives? Perhaps it's the thought that a son or daughter is moving on to create a new life and a new family. Whatever feelings a wedding evokes, videos are almost certain to play a major role in capturing the emotions and the love that are a part of this once-in-a-lifetime occasion.

Unfortunately, too many wedding videos manage to miss the most important aspect of a wedding day—the family's feelings and emotions. Although months and months will be spent planning a wedding, on videotape the occasion too often comes out as being a one-day event. Since a wedding day is the culmination of so many plans, dreams, and emotions, the status quo isn't sufficient anymore. How can you honestly expect some hired strangers to show up at an appointed time and get all of those plans, dreams, and emotions on tape? Something more is needed. Namely, a sense of family.

One of the best wedding videos we have seen didn't even have any coverage of the wedding itself, which took place outdoors and in the evening. After the bride came down the aisle there wasn't enough daylight left to continue recording. The next thing we saw was the reception, and the rest of the tape continued from there. Now, this video was shot by a cousin of the bride and was never intended to be a wedding video. But what the cousin managed to capture was the feeling that an entire family was involved in the event. It didn't matter that we never saw the actual ceremony. We saw something equally important—a family celebrating the marriage of one of their own.

It's only when you look at an amateur video like this that you begin to notice what is missing from most "professional" wedding videos. Sure, you see beautifully taped ceremonies and highlights of the receptions. You see interviews, and congratulations from business associates and school friends. But where are the things that really matter? Where is the sense of family involvement? Of all the tapes we viewed in our research, it was only in those in which a close friend or family member did the interviewing that people loosened up with their feelings, thus making the wedding video genuinely special.

So, what should you do? How can you work it so you'll have a wedding video that's both professional and personal?

Give this easy solution some thought. Divide your wedding coverage into two parts, and let each receive the attention of those who know them best.

★ Let the hired professionals concentrate on their specialties: the wedding ceremony and the reception.
★ Let your family and friends take care of the rest—those videos that require a more personal and intimate touch.

When the wedding's over you'll have two video versions. Keep them separate or try editing the two together to make a video that's better than anything either party could have shot on its own.

DUAL WEDDING COVERAGE

There's a good reason for hiring a professional video team. It will bring something that you probably don't have—expertise in taping under all sorts of circumstances and the right kind of video equipment. So when it comes to the wedding, hire professionals. Let them supply the two or three camcorders and the rest of the fancy equipment—the right kind of microphones, tripods, and lights that you don't own. At the reception, let them be responsible for providing the framework coverage of the main events—the first dance, the speeches, the cutting of the cake—everything that is part of the event of the day.

But while they are working on the "bread and butter" framework of the day, a close family member will be supplying the "gravy" for the video. That person will be responsible for coverage that is every bit as important as the main events but all too often overlooked, the heart of your video—the personal, family side of the wedding day.

We've come up with a few ideas to help you create this personal style of wedding video. By using any of them, in conjunction with the tape provided by your professional team, you will be able to capture the true family flavor of any wedding. We're even willing to bet that once you get started you'll find even more areas that will be unique to your family's wedding.

FAMILY TOUCHES THAT THE PROFESSIONALS WON'T GET!

First of all you need to sit down for a minute and think about the big picture. Along with making decisions about the ceremony, guest lists, the reception, flowers, and so on, you need to think about the video coverage for your wedding. Remember, in every event we've discussed so far, we've stressed beginning-middle-end. The beginning of your tape will take you through the early planning stages of the wedding. Deciding upon the floral arrangements, the fitting sessions for the gown and tuxedos, the wedding rehearsal and the rehearsal dinner will be the middle. The end of your wedding video will be the wedding ceremony and the reception. Put these three pieces together and you'll have a great wedding package.

Once you have thought about the coverage you would like, it is time to find two or three people to help with the taping. Try not to scare them away by making this appear to be a major commitment. Ask a couple of friends or family members if they would be willing to come along on some of the planning sessions from time to time. If a friend is going gown shopping with you anyway, maybe she can do some taping too. The important point is, make sure that the person you ask to come along knows how to use your camcorder and will be comfortable in using it.

We know that most people are not in the habit of taping their prewedding plans, but a wedding season is full of videotape potential. Here you will find those family moments that a professional crew would never be able to tape. But since you and your family are there, you can record the emotional highs and tearful frustrations as the wedding plans come together and the big day nears.

PREWEDDING EVENTS TO COVER

Shopping for the Bridal Gown

Hardly anyone thinks about covering this task with a camcorder. Have a friend or sister come along and shoot some video of the bride-to-be modeling a couple of gowns. It's important to think fun here, so the more you catch of the interaction between those involved, the better.

Fitting Sessions

Complement your gown video with some shots of the fitting sessions. All you need is a bit of video to capture the memory of these occasions. Since you will probably find these sessions less fun than the gown shopping, keep your coverage short. Save your tape for the more exciting occasions to come.

Choosing Tuxedos

The guys may not have as much fun as the women do, but a couple of hoots can be found in tuxedo shops too. Look for the same type of coverage here as you did when shopping for a gown. Again, it's very important to have a close friend or family member along to shoot these videos for you. There's a lot of fun to be found here and it takes a lighthearted friend to shoot these videos and bring out the best in everybody.

Checking the Location of the Ceremony

Consider bringing someone along to shoot a little video of the bride and groom's first walk-through of the wedding location. Wherever the ceremony will take place, there's usually a first meeting with a wedding coordinator and a tour of the facility. The person shooting these videos may have more luck if she simply adopts the role of an observer. Video of this will provide a nice memory.

Wedding Rehearsal

The most important thing to avoid is offending the presiding official. The rehearsal is a semiserious occasion that has a lot of potential for contributing to a fun video. Inform the presiding official ahead of time that you would like to record some of this. Presumably she will cooperate as long as the person shooting the videos doesn't distract people from the task at hand.

Rehearsal Dinner

Traditionally, after the wedding rehearsal there's a dinner party. This is a wonderful, informal occasion where everybody who is involved in the wedding is in a happy and relaxed mood. "Informal" seems to be the key here so what you should try to capture is a brief sampler of all of the people in attendance. Pass the camera around and have other people shoot a few seconds here and there too. As long as you keep looking for the fun and the laughter you'll have a video that can't be beat.

Interviewing Bride and Groom About Preparations

Treat this like any other interview but in a relaxed, lighthearted way. You're not after any earth-shattering revelations, only their feelings and thoughts. Ask questions like:

★ Is it still fun?
★ Are you going to make it to the wedding day?
★ Are all the family members still speaking to one another?

You get the idea. It's your interview; you come up with the questions.

At-Home Preparations on Wedding Day

Don't say it. You think we're crazy, right? As if there isn't enough commotion already! Nevertheless, dig out your camcorder and record some of the prewedding panic attack, for this is just the sort of thing you will love having on videotape (if you survive the wedding). Whoever is the designated camera operator for this stuff will need to get himself ready first. Once ready, he should feel free to wander around and poke into everybody else's preparations. Some great moments to capture, by merely letting the camera observe, are the bride getting ready (but don't impose on her), and a view or two of her gown before she dresses.

Arrivals at Church and Last-Minute Fixes

It may help if you keep reminding yourself that you're just shooting a behind-the-scenes video of a wedding. What you should look for are bits and pieces of all the goings on before the wedding. Keep an eye open for those last-minute preparations of both bride and groom. Little things like straightening the tie, last-minute pep talks, arranging the bride's headpiece, her last-minute touchups. Remember, all of this will be forgotten in a couple of months unless you record some of it now.

Point-of-View Shots from Audience's Perspective

Now we're getting into an area that you probably would have covered anyway. Since you're at the wedding and have a camcorder, why not grab some shots of the procession down the aisle? Your coverage should give everyone an idea of how it felt to be in the audience while the wedding was going on. Pick a good spot from which to shoot—the best position is usually directly in a center aisle seat near the front. Be aware of the professionals shooting video and don't position yourself so as to block their view. Just get a nice pan shot of the groom coming down the aisle and taking his place, then do the same for the bride.

Family Reactions and Comments after Ceremony

Since the bride and groom are usually the first ones to leave the ceremony, everyone else is left with a few minutes to stand around and chat. The main event is over and a sense of relief should be evident. This is the time to grab a couple of moments with some of the immediate family. Mothers and fathers might be your first targets, but don't overlook brothers or sisters or anyone else especially close to the bride and groom. Keep these video bits short and lighthearted.

Bride and Groom's Ride to Reception

Here's crazy idea number two. Has anyone done this before and if not, why not? Who knows what goes on in the back of that limousine on the ride to the reception? If the new couple are really into home videos, consider putting a camcorder in the limousine with them. If they feel like shooting a little video of each other during the ride, they can. Maybe it'll turn into something and maybe it won't. But, hey, it's worth the try!

Informal Arrival at Reception

What you now want to look for is some video of the bride and groom before they make their entrance into the reception. Something of their arrival, their leaving the limo, and perhaps their walking through the lobby on their way to the reception hall. What you're seeking is a nice little piece to complement the professional coverage (which will probably show them leaving the wedding, then instantly walking into the reception).

Personal, Family Thoughts During Reception

This is the area in which a professional wedding video will most likely come up short. You can easily remedy this shortcoming because you know all the family members and the professionals don't. There are two ways to go about getting this coverage and the decision is up to you. You may walk around with your own camcorder and do some quick, fun interviews with some of those closest to the bride and groom. Or you (or a close family member) may walk around with the video professionals and act as a liaison between them and the wedding family. In either case, what you are trying to avoid is the sterility that results when total strangers try to interview each other.

Come up with something different, something a shade more personal than "What did you think of the wedding?" or "Do you have any thoughts for the bride and groom?" Instead, ask questions like:

★ Tell us a funny story about the bride that the groom might not know about (and vice versa).
★ Give us a prediction—what do you think the bride and groom will be doing five years from today?
★ (For a relative.) What made the bride (or groom) special as a small child? Adolescent? Young adult?
★ (For friends.) How did the bride and groom let you know that they had decided to marry.
★ What makes the bride and groom each happiest? How do you think they can keep their marriage happy?
★ How will the bride and groom celebrate their fiftieth wedding anniversary?

Here's another trick to get people to loosen up. Instead of asking questions from off camera, have someone be an on-camera interviewer. This way she can go right up to Uncle Frank and Aunt Tilly, put her arms around them, and ask questions that are really close to home.

Bride and Groom Leaving for Honeymoon

If you have been the one shooting videos all this time, congratulations are in order. Not only have you given an entire day to the bride and groom, but you've paced yourself so you're still functioning at the end of the reception too.

A nice closing piece to the wedding-reception video is a shot of the bride and groom getting into their car and leaving the reception to a chorus of waves and goodbyes. After that, the day's about over. If anything is still going on at the reception, you might shoot a bit of that. Or look for a nice closing shot to end it all—perhaps an invitation lying against an empty champagne bottle or the remains of the wedding cake. Whatever you come up with, congratulate yourself. You've put in a long day.

One additional note. If a wedding is looming on the horizon in your family or in your circle of friends, volunteering to tape the pre-wedding plans is an excellent gift. You might specify: "I'll tape a day of shopping for gowns, a day of looking at reception locations, registering for gifts, one meeting with the clergyperson [or whoever will perform the ceremony], the final gown fitting, and the rehearsal dinner." Any bride and groom in the world will be thrilled to have this lovely one-of-a-kind gift.

13
SCHOOL AND CHURCH PROGRAMS

AVE YOU been to a children's program at a school or a church lately? A school play, choir program, church play, or any other children's presentation must have more camcorders per square foot than a camcorder warehouse. If a hundred children are in the program, seventy-five adults will be holding video cameras, all vying for coveted taping positions. Even the Superbowl makes do with only fifteen to twenty cameras (including the blimp).

Several elements are at work here. First, you're not the only person who will want to tape the program. Second, you will be taping in an auditorium, church, or multipurpose room that may not be lighted for video. Third, you're slightly nuts if you think that anyone in your family will ever want to watch the entire school or church program more than once. Think highlights. And fourth, you will miss the whole show if you're too busy jockeying for position and counting down the moments until your child makes an appearance or sings a song.

We've laid out some guidelines to follow for taping any school or church program. The main point is, be considerate of others, including those in the production and those in the audience. It may be wise to check beforehand with the person in charge about any policy on videotaping the program. The remaining basic guidelines are:

★ *Arrive early to pick out a location.* The first three rows or the front row of the balcony should be sufficient. The good-sport rule is, if you don't get to the auditorium or hall early enough, accept your lot and do the best you can. Don't take a seat and then slowly inch your way up the aisle during the performance.

★ *Don't block the view of others.* Owning a camcorder does not give you a sacred right to videotape something at the expense of others. In fact, if you are at an event without your equipment, notice how downright irritating some people can be with their cameras, still and video. It is never all right simply to stand up and begin taping. Our opinion is the only appropriate place for standing is at the back of the auditorium or in the balcony (provided patrons aren't seated there). Standing on the sides may give you a good picture, but it is still very distracting to the seated audience. And if there is a horde of parents with cameras, it's extremely distracting to the people who are performing. Which leads us to . . .

★ *Don't distract from the event.* Once you're seated, stay seated. Don't get up, scoot around, or change seat positions unless there is a natural break or intermission. Don't have auxiliary lights going on and off as you discover certain portions of the program don't have the light level you'd like. We would also caution against a general boorish behavior—just because your child isn't performing in a certain section doesn't mean that you can take that time to move around, test lights, or perfect your camera angle. Have some respect for the entire production.

It goes without saying, the quality of the sound you will record will be less than ideal. At best you'll probably be picking up the sound from speakers that are set up for a large hall. To record the best audio possible, you'll need to be close to a speaker or, if possible, run a separate microphone with cable from the speaker or public address system. If you plan to do the latter, check beforehand to see if everything is compatible—two minutes before the performance is not the time to try and set this up.

Other ways to get what you want on tape:

★ If you have the option, tape the dress rehearsal. Of course, you'll need to get permission from the appropriate person first. You will probably be able to move around more freely at a dress rehearsal than at the final performance.

★ Do you have a friend with a camcorder who also has a child in the same program? If so, divide up sections of the program, then dub copies of each other's tape. You probably won't have to dub the whole thing, but your friend might have had a better angle than you had for some important parts.

★ We spoke to a person who told us that her child's school arranged to have someone videotape the annual program. Tapes were then sold as a fundraiser for the school. Perhaps you can arrange a similar setup. Most schools have video equipment available and plenty of student volunteers that could help you put the entire production together.

TAPING A SCHOOL PLAY

The Opening: Preparation for the Play

Begin your tape at home as the child or children excitedly prepare to leave for the school. You might question the children as a TV interviewer would: "Are you excited about opening night?" "Do you think the play will have a long run?" "Any thoughts before we see you onstage?"

The Body: Covering the Play

You might set the scene once you get to the school ("We're at the auditorium awaiting the beginning of Ryan's class production of *Peter Pan*. Excitement fills the air."). As the lights go down and the play begins, record the opening scene. Depending on where your child is in the play, try to get a few scenes before and after his appearance. Capturing the whole play on tape is not what you're after. If you tape a little you'll enjoy a lot.

The Closing: After the Play

As you're leaving, tape reactions from parents and siblings like a theater reviewer ("Do you think it will make it to Broadway?" "What about that tension in the second act?" "Did you see any award-winning performances?"). You should also tape the children after the play since they'll probably still be excited from the experience—"How did it feel to be onstage?" "Did you like acting?" "What was the most fun?" "How did it feel to hear the applause for the play?" You might think of a question to end the piece: "Any final thoughts about tonight's performance?" Or if your family has planned an after-play treat or party, use that as an end: "We're having frozen yogurt and still talking about the great play we saw tonight. Any final words from our star?"

Remember, as you would for most other special occasions, you're taping to enhance the memory of the event, not to document it all minute by minute. And even though your tape will certainly be fun to watch, your child needs to know that you sat with rapt attention as he was onstage and said his lines or sang his song. So get a bit of the performance on tape, then set the camera down and be a doting parent.

14
CHILDREN'S
SPORTING EVENTS

S THERE ONE PARENT in the world who has a camcorder, a child playing sports, and doesn't have hours of tape covering all the "big" games? From what we see of children's sporting events, every parent with a camcorder has a full video library of every catch, every hit, and every meet-winning performance. Should your child become another Wayne Gretzky or Chris Evert, the world will forever be in your debt. Historians will have a field day analyzing every sports video you shot. Unfortunately, most of the eighty million children who play sports don't become famous athletes, so their parents are left with hours of sports videotapes that nobody wants to watch.

So we have a dilemma. As parents we want to document our child's sporting activities but on the other hand, we don't want to end up with a small library of monotonous videocassettes. Sure, all those big games are important, but how do you manage to shoot just a portion of an activity that lasts for hours at a time and is spread over weeks, even years? The way we view it you have only two realistic choices:

133

Choice 1. You can take your camcorder along and record every minute of every event. Then you can take all those cassettes and edit them into a highlights package. After only a couple hundred hours of work you'll have a perfect reel filled with nothing but the greatest moments of soccer, swimming, baseball. . . .

Choice 2. More simply, instead of recording everything, shoot your videos selectively. Pick out a sample game or event and be happy with the coverage you get. Anything that you happen to miss—either that day or on one when you didn't tape—you can re-create by using interviews with or reenactments by those involved. There's a bonus when you choose this method. Now you'll be able to enjoy some of these events without being a slave to your camcorder.

For the rest of this chapter, we will walk you through the steps and show you how to make your own highlights tape. You'll learn how you and your camcorder can capture the best of your child's sporting days without going through a whole lot of trouble. You will not be taping every single game, but we promise that you will end up with a great tape, one that captures the feeling of your child's participation in organized sports along with the highs and lows accompanying it.

THINK SPORTS STORY

Pick a sport, any sport, and the basic framework for covering it on video is essentially the same. That each game is played differently doesn't matter because basically you are still telling a story, as you did for your vacation video or your Christmas Day video, only here the story is the event itself.

We have repeatedly stressed how each story needs a beginning, a middle, and an end. Your sports video should be no different. The beginning of your story will be the preparation for the game or event, warmups, and pregame interviews. The middle, or body, of your story will encompass your child's participation in the event. The end of your story will be postgame scenes and interviews. Be it swimming, football, baseball, or track, what you're after is the same basic story every time—your child and how he fits into the game.

COVERAGE—TEAM OR INDIVIDUAL?

All sports break down into one of two categories—team or individual. Team sports will require from you a little more effort on your part to create an interesting, personal video simply because other players are involved. A team consisting of six, nine, or even twenty-two members makes it very difficult to focus all the attention on just your child. An individual sport, on the other hand, has the opposite problem. Here you'll need to work at conveying the feeling that your child is still part of a school team, that her individual performance still falls within the framework of a team competition. The sports you cover will have different names but you'll always seek the same result—individual and intimate coverage of your child performing as part of a larger body.

Before you drag your child and camcorder off to the playing fields, ask yourself three questions:

Question 1—How much of this event do I want on videotape?

At the very most, set a self-imposed limit on yourself of covering no more than three events per season. If your child is very good at his or her particular sport, you'll lean toward the higher side of our limit. On the other hand, if your child has average ability or is a beginner, maybe you should consider shooting only a sampler of a single game. There's a huge difference between being the star of the team and being a benchwarmer. If your child's ability improves during the season, you can always return and shoot another event. Nobody wants memories that last forever if they consist only of sitting on the bench or striking out each time at bat. Be aware of your child's feelings toward the sport and make your decision accordingly. The best sports videos will be of your child playing and having a good time.

Question 2—How close is my child to her team and teammates?

If your child has several close friends on the team or if the team is almost a second family to her, you will want to expand your video coverage to include the other team members. Usually we are biased toward our own children; but if several other teammates are important to your child, you will want to include them as well. Instead of shooting a video that's 80 percent your child and 20 percent the rest of the team, balance things out to an even fifty-fifty. Watching your child's best friend make a catch can be just as pleasurable as watching your own.

Question 3—Is the tape strictly for me and my family or will I be shooting a game-type video for the team to analyze?

The type of coverage that you shoot will vary according to your viewing audience. If the tape is for your own personal use, then feel free to shoot as much of your child as you like. But if others are to watch your videos, you will need to be more balanced in your coverage. If it's for the team, then the whole team should be covered. If it's for one or two other families, then cover their children as evenly as you cover your own.

GENERAL RULES FOR VIDEOTAPING ANY SPORT

1. *Use a tripod.* If you want your videos to appear halfway decent, they must be steady. Nobody can hand-hold a camcorder for three hours and still keep a steady shot, especially when it is zoomed in all the way. Hand-held shots are great for the closeups you'll also be getting, but as for the game itself, you will need a tripod.

2. *Bring extra batteries.* The typical camcorder battery lasts twenty minutes; the typical team sport lasts two hours. Which one will run out first? Be sure you have at least two fully charged batteries every time you go out to shoot. If you're really serious about covering team sports, consider buying an auxiliary battery pack. These are larger, heavier, and usually come with a shoulder strap or belt, and can last up to eight hours on a charge. One auxiliary battery will get you through an entire day of shooting and still be able to power your portable TV during the trip home.

T I P

To conserve battery power, be frugal in your use of the camcorder's zoom lens. The motor that drives the zoom mechanism uses a lot of power. Therefore, if you have the option, try zooming the lens by hand until you are ready to record.

3. *Use a telephoto extender for your camcorder.* Look into purchasing a 1.5x, 2x, or even a 5x extender to attach to your camcorder's lens. These adaptors will enable you to zoom in much more closely to your subject than you can with just a standard camcorder lens. For most events you will probably be some distance away from the action, so a telephoto extender can make this distance seem less apparent. Always remember: the closer you can make your videos appear, the more interesting they will be. That may be your child on the screen, but who can tell if he's so far away you need subtitles to point him out?

4. *Rent or buy a narrow-pattern microphone.* Your camcorder's standard microphone is fine for the closeup work you'll be doing but it won't pick up much of the action if you're 100 feet away. Narrow-pattern microphones perform the same kind of function as a telephoto lens—they enable you to zoom in on more specific sounds. A narrow-pattern microphone still won't put you right in the middle of the team, but the sound quality will be much better than what your standard camcorder microphone would pick up.

5. *Keep all of your sporting tapes separate.* Don't mix baseball games with birthday parties by combining them on one tape. By keeping sports separate from the rest of the family's events, you will have a much better record of your child's performances. Each season as well as each sport should have its own dedicated tape.

T I P

An important point to know in taping all sporting events, is that closeups emphasize positive memories. Too many Closeups of a losing effort will serve only to reinforce the negative memories your child has of the day. If he wins, closeups are great; if not, temper the moment by staying wide.

Now that we've warmed you up with a few tips and asked you to make a couple of decisions, it's time to get down to the individual sports. Before you go out to shoot for the first time, review the section for that particular sport, then refresh yourself with the standard rules we've suggested for every event. After you've shot an event, go back and look at the video with a critical eye. If you don't like the way things came out, go back and try it again. There is only one way to learn and that is by doing. Even if it takes you two or three times, it's the end result that's important. Ten years from now nobody will remember that your first attempt wasn't so hot.

COVERING TEAM SPORTS

FOOTBALL

Football is one of those sports in which a person spends much more time practicing than playing. Your child may spend two hours a day, five days a week practicing, but less than three hours a week actually playing the game.

Since practice is a huge part of the football season, make an effort to stop by and record part of a workout. Your child will remember these sessions as vividly as games so it's only fair that they get coverage as well. Be sure to discuss your plans with the coach ahead of time and promise you'll be unobtrusive while taping.

After you arrive at the practice field, look for individual workouts. Keep an eye open for the coach too, as you'll probably discover that he has a personality that's unique to practice sessions. At the same time keep an ear open for the instructions being yelled out by the rest of the coaching staff. (We hope it's family-rated language.) Remember, the voices and instructions you record will be as memorable as the images themselves.

Deciding upon which game to record is more important than you may realize. Choose not only a game your team is favored to win, but also one in which your child is expected to get a lot of playing time. This advice may seem a bit underhanded but it applies to any sport you'll cover. We'll say it again. If these are to be the memories of a lifetime, it doesn't hurt to make them winning memories.

Pregame Coverage

For a moment think about all the televised football coverage you've seen in your life. Each game has its own story, doesn't it?

There's always a setup, maybe something about the key players—who's injured, who's expected to play well—then the game itself. You can actually duplicate the same sort of coverage even though you'll be limited by having only one camera.

Before the game begins, set things up by first shooting an introduction, then some of the pregame activities. Your introduction should be simple. It can even be as basic as shooting the scoreboard to show the names of the two teams. Do a voice-over at the same time, saying something like: "We're here tonight at Westchester High School to cover the battle between the Westchester Vikings and the Raleigh Knights. It's Saturday night, October fifteenth, and it looks as if we're in for quite a matchup." After you've completed the introduction, look for interesting shots of the players preparing for the game—perhaps some closeups of players doing their stretching exercises or team units running through their play drills.

Game Coverage

When you feel that you have enough for a nice opening, grab your tripod and get set up for the kickoff. The best location for shooting a football game is on the fifty-yard line. It always helps to have some height, though, so find a clear spot near the top of the bleachers. If your stadium doesn't have bleachers, try using a stepladder or arrange to stand on the back of a pickup truck. Height is crucial to videotaping the game, so be greedy and take every foot you can get.

If the spot you end up with isn't ideal and runs the risk of getting blocked by people, talk it over with them ahead of time. Most people will be considerate about not blocking your shot if you will only take a moment and ask them not to. Once you have a prime spot and a clear view, you are ready for the game.

If you watch much football on TV you may have noticed a distinct pattern in the coverage. For most games only one or two cameras cover the game itself. The other cameras merely add detail to that basic coverage. What you and your camcorder will attempt is to copy that game camera coverage because (1) that is what you're interested in and (2) you have only one camera.

The basic camera shot for any football play starts with the players that make up the offensive and defensive lines. Then, as the play develops, the camera simply follows the action. If your camcorder has a long enough zoom lens, feel free to tighten up the shot a little as the runner carries the ball or the quarterback throws a pass. Now you may quit right here and keep repeating this same shot or you may vary it periodically. A second alternative is starting the play on a closeup of the quarterback and then zooming out as the play develops. A third alternative is to start very wide, including all the receivers, then zooming in more tightly as the play starts and runs its course.

If your child plays on the offensive or defensive line you'll want to shoot some of the confrontation between him and his immediate opponent. The best way to cover this is on a tighter shot of just the small group of players around him. Tape one or two plays like this, then revert back to general game coverage. Periodically start each play wide, then zoom in on this little group. Don't forget the rest of the game and try to build excitement whenever you get the chance. When you're playing on the line, one play is a lot like the next, so twenty-five consecutive closeups won't make for a very interesting video.

If your child plays one of the more glamorous positions, in the backfield or as a receiver, you'll want to stick with game-action coverage. The reason is simple. When you're shooting game coverage and your child is involved in a play, you'll still see everything that happens. Tight, isolated coverage is okay once in a while, but if you stay with it too often you'll end up missing the rest of the action. It's best to try and create a feeling for the entire game by interspersing your game coverage with isolated coverage of your child.

While you're shooting, always be aware of maintaining the continuity of the game. To do this, all you need do is periodically shoot the scoreboard or the down markers so your viewer will have a feel for how the game is progressing. Often we get so wrapped up in shooting the game that we forget to keep track of the down, quarter, or time remaining. It won't ruin your coverage if you forget to do this, but it will enhance it if you remember to add it.

Don't drive yourself crazy by trying to shoot every play of the game. Before you start taping, decide which quarters you will tape and which ones you'll sit out and enjoy the game.

After you have shot some of the opening series of plays, walk down to the sidelines and shoot from there for a while. Look for some of those great hand-held shots that you see on TV all the time. Feel free to steal some of the professional's ideas; shoot the coaches, players, fans, and cheerleaders. Try a couple of arty shots at ground level or some walking shots of a pacing coach.

Postgame Coverage

Be sure you are at field level when the game ends. This is the time for those all-important closeups of tired, exuberant players. (We hope they're tired winners.) Record some hugs and congratulations, and don't forget the consolation handshakes with the opposing team. As soon as you can, pick your child out of the mob and focus your coverage on him.

If you were unlucky enough to have missed any big plays, try to get your child or a teammate to describe them for you. A firsthand reenactment of a touchdown catch or a blocked punt is nearly as good as seeing it. If you were fortunate enough to capture a big play, have your child describe that for you too. It's the moment of victory you want to capture, so grab as much video as you can while the memories are fresh.

There you have it—one game in the life of a football player. The key to it all is simple: tell a story. If you missed a few pages of one chapter, make up for it with a P.S. or a reenactment.

BASEBALL

When your child decides that baseball is his number one favorite sport, there is only one thing you can do: accept the fact that your videos will be long and fairly dull. We will show you some tricks that will make them as interesting as possible, but unless you decide to edit each game into a highlights package, resign yourself to accepting the dull along with the exciting.

To avoid redundancy, we will go over only the points that make your coverage of baseball different from that of other sports. You still need to tell a story and it should be intimate. As far as the game itself goes, keep following the ball and let it bring you to the play. Also, keep an eye open for any closeups or new camera angles that may look interesting.

Game Coverage

Some of the things that slow the pace of baseball can actually work to your advantage in making a nice video. Since the players don't change position all that much, you can even get away with skipping a couple of innings. One inning looks much like the next so if you do stop for awhile, be sure to voice-over the inning and the outs when you start recording again.

Furthermore, since many baseball fields offer little in the way of grandstands or spectator seating, more than likely you will be shooting most of your videos from field level. If this is your situation, choose the side of the field closest to your team's dugout and set up your position just past either first or third base.

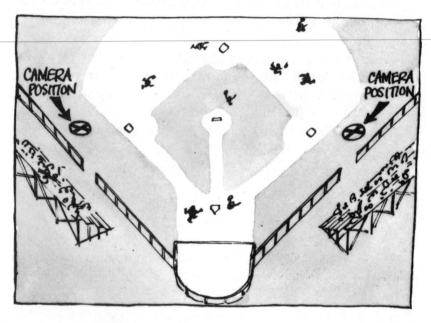

In fact, the best position to have is on the field, inside the fences. Of course, like most creative people, you may suffer a little for your art. If you are inside the protective fences, be aware that you risk being hit by a foul ball or interfering with a popup. When you cover baseball, your best defense is to keep an eye on the ball at all times, especially when a batter is up.

Whether on the field or outside the fences, you will have a few choices for camera shots:

Choice 1. A shot that includes both the pitcher and the batter at the same time. This will allow you to see both sides of the action, then to follow the ball when it is hit.

Choice 2. A tighter shot of only the batter and the catcher. The pitched ball will enter your shot and if it's hit, either follow the batter or pan quickly to where the ball has been hit.

Choice 3. A tight shot of the pitcher, quickly panning with the ball to the home-plate area. Again, if the ball is hit, you must choose to follow either the runner or the ball.

Of our three choices, number one works best for providing good, basic coverage of the game. It allows you to see both the pitcher and the batter, and makes it easier to follow the ball should it be hit. Choices two and three are fun to try once in a while, but only as a break from the regular coverage. As in any other sport, if you whip pan too quickly, the viewer will find it difficult to tell what is going on. Wider shots provide plenty of information and are much less dependent upon the skill of the cameraperson.

Unlike those of some sports, the natural sounds you'll hear during a baseball game will add immeasurably to your coverage. Since the action of the game may be, shall we say, "lacking" at times, fieldside chatter and "atta boys" will contribute a lot to the feel of having been there. Your standard camcorder microphone is perfect for this because you're in close and the sounds are coming equally from all directions. This is an instance where you want to hear the players on the bench, the third baseman, the opposing team, and the fans.

There is one point to consider. If your ears hear a sound, your eyes will want to see the source. If you can hear the players on the bench jabbering away, include a couple of shots that show them in full voice. The same goes for the crowd, or any razzing by the opposing bench. A simple rule is: If you can hear it, show it.

Since you will need to show some of these "atmospheric" sound makers, try some different camera shots while you are doing it.

★ Instead of standing in one spot and grabbing cutaway shots of anything that looks interesting, put your legs to work and take a walk. Get closer to your subject.

★ Instead of a boring shot of the players on the bench yelling "Get a hit!" shoot across them so we can see the team and the batter at the same time.

A variety of quick shots from different angles will increase the pacing and build excitement in any video.

★ Instead of a static crowd shot or your standard pan from face to face, go over to the crowd and shoot a couple of closeup faces. Once you've done the closeups, shoot across them so you can see the playing field.

Any of these methods will let you tie together the actions on the field with those on the sidelines.

Voice-overs

Something else to keep in mind is doing voice-over announcements—verbal reminders informing the viewer who is at bat, on base, or whatever.

There seem to be two approaches here; both are valid so the decision lies with you. Some feel that after you've spent a season covering a team the names of everybody on it are ingrained in your memory forever. Therefore, there's no need to keep mentioning that Ryan Michaels is at bat because you and your child will never forget Ryan's name. The other side of the coin is that you will eventually forget the names of most of the teammates. In five years you may have trouble remembering all of them and in ten you may forget even the coach's name.

From past experience, we tend to side with those who predict forgetfulness. You don't need to mention the name of every person you shoot, but you should announce the player's name at least once or twice during the game. Just a simple announcement, like, "Ryan Michaels is up and the count is two balls and one strike"; or, "Tim Hoover is on second, with two outs." Should you forget their names in ten years or so, a single voice-over will refresh your memory for another ten.

Pacing the Action

As the game progresses try some of the techniques we discussed in Chapter 3 to build excitement. You can easily increase the pace of the action by shooting shorter-length shots and including more cutaways. If it's the bottom of the ninth with two outs and the winning run at third, show the excitement. Shoot some quick shots of the pitcher, the baserunner, the bench, and the crowd, then settle on the big confrontation between pitcher and batter. After each pitch shoot another quick cutaway, then return to the action. If you're lucky, something exciting will happen and you'll have a great finish to your tape. If you're not so lucky and your team loses, you'll still have a great tape because your shooting technique will have helped capture the emotional intensity of a closely fought contest.

Remember, it's how you shoot the game that makes it boring or interesting. By using a combination of different shots and a quick-cutting technique, you can make any game look like a life or death duel.

BASKETBALL

Videotaping a basketball game unearths a new set of challenges. Although there are some similarities with football coverage (both take place on a rectangular surface and the action goes in both directions), basketball is simultaneously easier and more difficult to cover. The problem that usually arises—making things more difficult—is managing to find a camera position high enough to see all the action yet remains unblocked by the crowd.

Gymnasiums are fairly small to begin with, and when they are crowded, it often becomes difficult to find a good spot. The ideal camera position, as with most team sports, is in the middle of the sideline area and as high as possible. Usually this position is near the top of the bleachers on the center aisle. The crowd will still block your view every so often but usually it will be clear. If you have the luxury of time and can arrange to arrive at the gym early, set up your tripod and use it to reserve a good position. Once you stake out an area, people will usually be cooperative and try to stay out of your way.

What makes taping a basketball game easier is that the basic camera coverage is much simpler than that of football or baseball. To cover the game well, all you need to be concerned with is covering a 120-foot court where the action reverses direction every half minute or so. Every professionally televised basketball game uses just one camera to cover the game action; the others merely complement the coverage. All you will need to do is the same thing. Just follow the action up and down the court.

Game Coverage

When covering the game action keep the shot wide enough to let the play develop, then zoom in a little as the action moves to the key area and the basket. After a basket, follow the players bringing the ball up the court, widen to see the play develop, then tighten as the action nears the basket. Repeat this pattern for as long as you wish; it will give you good, solid basketball coverage.

Of course, you probably will not want to tape the entire game, so here's where a slightly different pattern will work. The only new variable you'll introduce to your game coverage is a cutaway shot now and then. Here's how it works:

★ Game-action coverage for a couple of baskets.
★ Stop recording.
★ Cutaway shot of the scoreboard showing score, period, and time.
★ Stop recording.
★ More game coverage.
★ Stop recording.
★ Scoreboard cutaway.
★ Game coverage.
★ Etc.

The added cutaway shots will bring continuity to your coverage. Now you can stop recording for as long as you like and the game will still make sense. Remember, if your last shot was of the game action, your next shot should be of the scoreboard, and vice versa. If you omit the cutaways, your viewers will have no idea of where they are in the game, what the score is, and how much time is left. Cutaway scoreboard shots are crucial if you want the game to make sense.

The nicest thing about covering basketball is that all ten players are in on the action most of the time. You can still shoot isolated coverage of your child's playing, but mostly you should stick with the general game action. You may use tighter shots of your child as cutaways, in addition to shots of the scoreboard, but these work best during time-outs and foul shots. The same goes for cutaways of the coach, bench area, and crowd.

Basketball games, unlike many other sports, will provide little opportunity for you to shoot from the floor. The small size of most gyms has a lot to do with this. In addition, some school regulations may actually forbid spectators from standing near the court.

If you are allowed to shoot some of the game from the floor, do it. You won't be able to see the action quite as well but the change in perspective will add visual interest. The main reason for shooting from the floor is to get closeups—of the coach, the teammates, the cheerleaders, the crowd, and especially the players. If regulations allow, position yourself as close to the basket as you can and shoot a low-angle shot of your team driving for a score. The networks get a lot of mileage from this type of shot, so why not borrow it?

Postgame Coverage

As the game draws to a close, make it a point to be at floor level. When the game is over, shoot some obligatory congratulations and handshakes all the while focusing most of the attention on your child. If you can get close enough to talk with the players, ask them a question or two about the game. All you need is a comment that conveys their feelings about the day. Temper your questions and comments to the outcome of your child's team. When everything is over and the gym is emptying out, remind yourself to get a shot of the scoreboard. If your team has won, that final score will be an essential part of your videotape memory.

SOCCER

Soccer is rapidly rising in popularity as a sport for girls and boys of all ages. If your household's sport is soccer, you will have to accept one little fact of life. Since even the television professionals have a difficult time covering soccer, you—with your one little camcorder—aren't going to shoot a spectacular video unless you happen to get very lucky. The reasons for this are many, not the least of which is that soccer is a game of finesse and endurance, neither of which is easy to convey on video. Still, we will show you how to cover the game as well as possible, and if you're lucky you may even capture a goal or two.

Videotaping soccer is no different from any of our other field sports: you may still record the entire game in the hopes of catching some great action, or you may shoot parts of the game and then re-create anything big you missed.

We are still dealing with a team sport played on a rectangular field, so much of the coverage we used for football applies here. The best position for you and your camera is still at midfield and, as always, the higher the better. There's a new twist to consider, though: most of a soccer game consists of players running up and down the field, and that alone doesn't make for an exciting video. So you will have to resort to a few camera tricks to create some visual interest. Before we get into that part, though, let's start at the beginning.

Pregame Coverage

The introduction to your soccer video should follow the same format we outlined for football. First set up the match by shooting a few pregame warmups and routines. Then, once you've gotten a minute or so of that, get into position for the start of the game. If you can't find a good spot at midfield, pick one that's close to the position your child is playing. This way you'll be right there if anything exciting happens.

Game Coverage

As the game begins the only camera rule you need remember is to follow the ball. Set up your shot so that it is wide enough to follow the ball and include the player action that accompanies it. As the game progresses and you become more comfortable with following the action, tighten up your shot so that you only see three or four players at a time. It will require quicker reflexes on your part to follow the action that tightly, but after a few minutes of practice it should become much easier. If for some reason you aren't able to get a camera position any higher than field level, stick with slightly wider coverage of the game.

Many of your shooting decisions will depend on the skill level of the children playing. Beginning players spend much of the game kicking the ball back and forth, so if your shots are too tight you'll end up with a lot of distracting whip pans. If your kids are at this level, stay loose, cover the action, and try the tighter shots only when the action is moving directly toward or away from you. As the children's skill level improves and their actions become more predictable, then start tightening your coverage. For example, when the ball is being worked down a sideline toward you, that's a great opportunity for a tight action shot.

Speeding Up the Action

Here is where we can use a couple of our editing-as-you-shoot lessons to speed up the action. The key that will make this trick work is keeping the game action going in the same direction for each drive on goal.

Here's what we mean. For illustration purposes, let's assume the ball is moving from left to right.

★ After you have followed the game action for a few seconds and your team is still moving the ball left to right, look for a slow moment and stop recording.
★ Frame up a tighter shot of your child and the one defending her. As soon as they begin moving left to right—it doesn't have to be the same drive on goal you were shooting a moment ago—start recording again. If your child gets the ball while you're shooting, count yourself lucky. If not, record her jockeying for position for a few seconds, then stop tape again.
★ Loosen back out to your follow-the-ball shot, wait for the action to resume left to right, then start rolling.

As long as you keep the screen direction of the ball moving left to right, all the action will look as if it occurred during the same drive on goal. In effect, what you have done is edit from a wide shot to a medium shot, then back to a wide shot while using only one camera. This trick will work for action moving in either direction; but you must remember, this is only an ideal situation.

However, if some exciting action starts but happens to be going in the opposite direction, go ahead and shoot it anyway. If the play ends up with a goal being scored, no one will care that the action appeared to be going the wrong way. If the play doesn't develop into anything, stop tape, then try our game plan once again.

After you have shot a few minutes of game action, take your camcorder off the tripod and move to the sidelines. This will be the other area where you'll need to "create" some visual excitement by coming up with some interesting camera shots. Because imitation is the sincerest form of flattery, feel free to copy any camera shot you see on TV. Always look for different angles from which to shoot:

★ Try a ground-level shot, or one that's over the shoulder of a player on the bench, of the action on the field.
★ Look for an offensive drive down the sideline that's headed toward the camera.

★ Start on a group of feet and the ball, then widen out as the play develops.

Shooting from the sidelines is the time to look for your closeups of players' faces, the bench, the coach, the crowd—anything to make the game more intimate. Shoot some of the game action, then shoot a face or two; shoot more game, then another face. Keep alternating your coverage between game action and cutaways, and you will create the impression that a lot is happening. When you do this well, your viewers will wonder where you got the extra camera.

Postgame Coverage

As the game draws to a close, it's best to be at field level so you can cover the postgame rituals. Look for the same things we covered in football and basketball, and look for your child so you can set up a postgame interview. If you feel you are agile enough, try walking and shooting as you ask your questions. Ask the children:

★ To give their impressions of the game and describe any big moments you may have missed.
★ About their opponents and if there were any moves they found difficult to keep up with.
★ To describe some of their moves that worked against their defenders.

The key here is to make it intimate. Their firsthand observations will add immeasurably to the you-were-there feeling that only the best videotapes convey.

As you can see our soccer coverage shares many similarities with the other sports we have discussed. We're still telling a story with a beginning, a middle, and an end. The key differences are the camera tricks we use to speed up the action and our ability to get close to the players so we can shoot great action closeups.

COVERING INDIVIDUAL SPORTS

In the introduction to this chapter we mentioned that there is a difference in how you cover individual sports from the way you cover team sports. Your coverage of a team sport should be balanced so that the team, as a whole, doesn't override the individual performance of your child. With an individual sport, though, you need to create the opposite effect—the feeling that your child is part of the team and not competing alone.

Here, unlike in team sports, it's very easy to isolate your child while he or she is swimming the 100-meter freestyle or performing a floor routine. In fact, most individual events take only a few minutes to complete so, in effect, each time you record you're creating a highlights package. The difficulty comes in trying to cover the other members of their team and the other teams entered in the meet. Therefore, that's what we will work on. First we will throw out a few ideas to make your individual coverage look better and then we'll review some techniques for tying it all together.

SWIMMING

If your child is interested in swimming the word *practice* won't come as much of a surprise: Since most of your child's life revolves around this word, why not cover one of those early-morning workouts? You're probably up anyway to drive her to the pool, right? So why not? Granted, practice sessions are pretty monotonous, but you don't need to shoot much of one to get the feel for what an entire session is like. Look for some coverage that will help create a slice-of-life piece of your child's average swimming day.

Shooting a Practice

Beginning: You should start your practice piece by shooting a low-angle wide shot of your child walking away from you and toward the pool or locker room. Keep this shot going for fifteen or twenty seconds and use it to set the mood for the rest of the practice.

Next, move into the pool area and look for another picturesque wide shot. Perhaps the sun rising through the trees. Then, pan to reveal the pool itself. The mood you are looking to set is one of quiet dedication, so any talking or voice-overs by you should be avoided. Your job is to be an observer, not a participant.

Middle: When you feel that you have captured the early-morning mood, look for some closeups of swimmers doing their laps. It won't take long for things to liven up a bit so don't feel that the entire piece needs to be silent and distant. If people start interacting with you while you are shooting, feel free to talk back, but try not to become an obvious part of the practice. All you are after is a feeling for what it is like to practice with the swim team every morning.

End: A five-minute piece is all you need and most of that should focus on your child doing the morning workout. To get a nice end to your practice piece, interview your child after the morning routine about how that day's workout went:

★ Did she feel good about the workout?
★ Is she working on a specific stroke?
★ How was her speed this morning?

Covering the Meet

When it comes to recording a swim meet, you're ahead of the game already. Since each event will be a small highlights package unto itself, all you have to do is find a good camera position and wait. If the events are relatively short-distance swims, you can get away with hand-holding the camera without much problem. For the longer races a tripod will allow you to shoot smoother, steadier videos. Either way, set yourself up near the center of the pool, preferably on the side closer to your child's lane.

Your basic swim-meet video should run something like this:

★ If there are introductions, shoot a tight shot of each swimmer, then pan to the next as she is introduced. Repeat this until you have covered all the competitors.
★ Stay with a fairly tight shot of two or three swimmers as they limber up and get positioned for the race.
★ As the starter gets them into position, widen your shot to include as many of the swimmers as you can.
★ Stay with a wide shot for the start of the race and while the contestants swim past you the first time.
★ The best time for zooming in for a closeup of your child is after the swimmers have made a turn and are coming back toward you.

If this is a fairly short event, four minutes or less, keep tape rolling for the entire race. Stay on a fairly wide shot most of the time so you can see the progression of the race. Avoid zooming in for a closeup more than once per lap. Your child is important, but, remember, you're trying to capture a feeling for the *race*. The focus on your child comes at the beginning and the end of the event.

As the swimmers approach the finish you'll need to make a decision on whether to keep shooting wide or tight. If your child is winning, or in tight competition for the lead, zoom in close and focus on her. If her competition is in an adjacent lane, include them both. Stay tight through the finish and record everything that happens. On the other hand, if your child isn't at the head of the pack, don't embarrass her with undue emphasis. Stay on a wider shot. It doesn't matter that you don't see who wins the race because that isn't important. What is important is staying with your child until the race is over.

Stop recording once the race ends, but keep an eye open for any positive activity that might take the sting out of losing—the coach or teammates coming over to offer condolences, things like that. If someone is coming over to your child, frame up a head-to-toe shot of him and start recording. Follow him as he heads toward your child, slowly zooming out to include everyone involved.

Emphasize the Team

There are numerous things you can shoot to make the day feel like the team effort it is. One is shooting closeups to create a sense of intimacy and participation. Some things to keep in mind:

★ The closer you can physically get to the swimmers, the more intimate your videos will appear.
★ Look for closeups of the team members as they watch one of the races and listen for the cheering and for the encouragement being yelled out.
★ If you can be next to the team during one of the races, try intercutting shots of the swimmers and the team.
★ Shoot a little of the race, then a bit of the team, and alternate for a minute or so to build a feeling of excitement for the event.

Other things to look for are crowd reactions, cutaway shots of the opposing swimmers, and strategy sessions with the coaches. Anything you can shoot that makes you feel as if you were part of the action will make for a great video.

GYMNASTICS

The same thoughts that apply to swimming coverage hold true for gymnastics. Consider videotaping a practice session, cover the meet as a team event, record each routine in its entirety, and try to create a feeling of intimacy.

The only change in coverage is that you will shoot in a gymnasium instead of poolside. It's still important to remember—

★ Shoot lots of closeups of the individual team members.
★ Include cutaways of the opposing team and the spectators.
★ Show the scoring, both individual and team.
★ Get closeups of the winners; show understanding for the runners-up.
★ Use a tripod for all your coverage of the routines.

TRACK AND FIELD

The principal drawback to videotaping track and field events is distance; you usually are some distance away from the action. The intimacy you can create in other sports videos is more difficult to duplicate here.

Covering the Meet

School regulations may not allow you to shoot from the field, so be prepared to shoot from the grandstand. As always, a tripod is a must for steady pictures. If you're a hundred yards away from the action you will need all the help you can get. In addition, you may want to consider using a narrow-pattern microphone. Without it you will have a difficult time hearing some of those distant sounds.

Wherever you end up shooting, when you're featuring track events apply the same shooting techniques we discussed for swimming. Cover the race on a wide shot and use tighter shots and closeups only to set the mood at the beginning and the end. Stay with your child, win or lose, and zoom in for tighter shots only once or twice during each race. In fact, tight shots will work only if the race is long enough, 400 meters or more, and then only on the back stretches. For shorter sprint races stay wide enough to see most of the competition.

For field events, a telephoto extender and a tripod are musts. Both will allow you to get better, closer shots of the action. Whenever it's physically possible to get nearer the individual events, do it. Position yourself so you can see your child's face as he sets up for each attempt and can see the landing area. It's the result of each attempt that's important, so be sure you see your child coming toward you each time.

Record each attempt in its entirety and be sure to shoot a cutaway of the height and distance marker at the end of each effort. After two or three rotations, you should also have a good idea of who his closest competitors are, so record one or two of their attempts as well. By including others, you will heighten the sense of competition and make it feel more like a team event.

Remember the advice we gave earlier: Tight shots for winners, wide shots for losers. If the event comes down to the final attempt and your child doesn't make it, don't linger on closeups of your discouraged athlete. You can dissipate his sense of loss by zooming out and looking for something else to cover. You be the judge, though. If he doesn't take losing well, don't linger.

One word of advice—even though your child's event is over, don't pack up your equipment and go home. This is still a team competition so there is always a chance your team may win the meet. A nice way to temper your athlete's losing effort is by putting more emphasis on the team's winning effort. Remember, look for the positive whenever you record sports, because these are the memories of a lifetime.

15

THANKSGIVING, EASTER, AND PASSOVER

THESE HOLIDAYS have two elements in common—food and family gatherings. They're holidays most families plan for, anticipate, and remember long after the day of celebration has come and gone. However, even though these are annual holidays, and even though they are important to families, we didn't find too many people who had actually taped the celebratory meals involved on these days. The memories of these meals are, after all, what we treasure.

Although taping a meal doesn't immediately come to mind when we think of an ideal videotaping opportunity, we would like to suggest that you try it at least once. How many times does your entire family, with a few extended members thrown in to boot, sit down at the dinner table to converse, celebrate, and eat? Not often, we'd bet. When it does happen, why not use your camcorder to capture a slice of it for posterity?

Think back to those Thanksgiving dinners at grandma's when you were a child. Wouldn't it be nice to have a ten-minute piece of just one you could look at today? We feel the same goes for Easter, Christmas, and especially the Passover Seder. Having a little video memory of any one of those meals would be wonderful. Well, now is the time to do it.

We think that a ten- or fifteen-minute video should be sufficient for most any occasion. Of course, there's nothing to prevent you from recording the entire meal if that's what you would like to remember. As always, we advise you to think highlights. When taping a meal, though, this does mean that whoever is in charge will be getting up and down frequently either to turn the camera on or to turn it off. You might follow this plan—five minutes at the beginning when people have just sat down, five minutes of midmeal conversation, and five minutes once dessert has been served.

We're assuming that since this dinner will be a special occasion the people in attendance will make an extra effort to be conversational. Now if this doesn't sound like your family, then maybe this isn't such a good idea for you. After all, no matter how special the occasion is, no one will want to watch a video of people sitting around a table and just eating. (But then, a tape of this type might be a hit in the video-as-art circuit—you might not watch it at home, but maybe some fringe experimental video group would be interested . . .) What we're after is the authentic slice of life that can be captured by trying something like this.

If you feel you will need to coax your family to be more interactive, try making this occasion into a video letter to someone who can't be there. Everyone should take a turn saying something to the missing person. After this, conversations should naturally start to flow.

If you're beginning to be persuaded that this could be a good idea, wait. It gets even better. Not only can you make this the memory of a lifetime; it's actually very easy to pull off. The key is making the taping an unobtrusive part of the meal. And what could be more unobtrusive than setting your camcorder on a tripod and leaving it there? All you need do is frame up a nice wide shot that includes everyone at the table, start rolling tape, then sit down and join in.

Of course, one wide shot probably won't enable you to see everyone clearly, but then, that doesn't necessarily matter. As long as you can see some part of everyone at the table, you won't have disembodied voices floating out of nowhere.

One thought to remember: when you're composing your wide

shot leave extra head room for any who may be standing from time to time. Just because someone goes to the kitchen to fetch more mashed potatoes doesn't mean he needs to be excluded from the shot. Frame up the whole table and leave plenty of room at the top.

Something else you may want to consider, especially if there are people who can't be seen clearly, and if you are taping the entire meal: change the camera's position after your first five-minute taping. Take a moment to get up and move everything to the opposite end of the table. Of course, you *will* remember to turn off the camera while you're moving it. Once the camcorder is in a new position, roll tape again. If after five minutes you still feel that you would like to continue recording, move the camera again. Since you don't have the option of adding closeups, changing angles is the only alternative for keeping your viewers interested.

Two other thoughts may help you keep this entire process as unobtrusive as possible. First, try and get away with using only the existing light at the table. If it is in fact too dark to make a decent picture and you must use an auxiliary light, then bounce the light off of the ceiling instead of shining it directly at the table. (See illustration on page 115.) By bouncing it you will obtain a much more natural look and avoid harsh shadows and squinting people. Comfortable people are happy people and happy people make for much better videos.

Second, take a moment to cover the camcorder's record-talley light with a piece of opaque tape. Some people become self-conscious when they know they are being taped and record-talley lights can contribute to that feeling. A camcorder that's merely sitting on a tripod soon becomes just another part of the meal, especially if there is nothing to indicate it is on. By taping over the lights you'll have one less thing to distract people from their meal. This tip is even more appropriate if your camcorder has an indicator light that flashes whenever tape is rolling.

If you're interested in taping some of the Passover Seder, making the taping process as unobtrusive as possible becomes your foremost thought. We can't count the number of people who have told us that they wished someone had recorded one of their childhood Seders, but that no one ever thought of it. Just because a meal centers around a religious occasion doesn't exclude it from quiet and tasteful taping.

If you plan to tape a Seder, the first thought you need to drop by the wayside is that of moving the camcorder every five minutes. When the occasion is more important than the coverage, things like changing the shot don't really matter. What you wish to capture is the quiet beauty of a family ritual. As long as you can see everyone in one shot and, most important, hear everything being spoken, then you have all you need.

Now for a sample Thanksgiving scenario.

THANKSGIVING

Think for a moment. What do you want to see in this video? How can we record the feeling of the holiday? The focus for the day should be that big meal, so everything you shoot should lead up to the moment when everyone sits down at the table. Well, what does everyone do several times during the day? They ask that age-old question, "When do we eat?" Why not have the video camera ask that question periodically throughout the day? The idea of sending the camera into the kitchen to check on preparations can help build the excitement of the video and the mood of the day.

For most of us, Thanksgiving is an indoor holiday. Be aware of the limitations of your lighting and don't forget to use auxiliary lights. Since you are planning on taping the meal, set up your tripod and check out your shots before your guests arrive. You may even have to rearrange some furniture in order to get the wide shot you'll need for the table. Stake out the tripod's claim to a corner and your claim to a seat near the camera.

Beginning: Start your video in the kitchen, with the preparation of the turkey. Voice-over that it's Thanksgiving and add the particulars about how you'll celebrate and who will be coming for dinner. Keep an ear open for comments from the children present; they're always fascinated with the sight of the turkey being prepared for roasting.

Middle: Pick up your recording of highlights once the guests start to arrive. Remember, you're aiming for short questions and answers, brief comments, and quick shots of kitchen preparations, table preparations, group conversations, children playing, and so on. Periodically poke your camera back into the kitchen for the when-do-we-eat update.

Are there a lot of children this year? Be sure to shoot some video at a child's eye level. Follow a child into the kitchen, holding the camera low for a child's point of view shot. Can the child see anything at all, or are there mysteries being performed at counter level? What is all the activity about and what does it all mean? The montage of all of these scenes will build to the day's main attraction, the meal.

End: As people begin to gather at the table, place your camera on the tripod. Once everyone has been seated, begin recording. You'll want to get the prayer or toast or whatever your family's Thanksgiving tradition may be. From here on, it's all up to you. If you have decided to tape the entire meal, check your watch once in a while so you can keep track of how long the camera has been recording from one angle. As we suggested before, vary the angle from time to time (whenever you can pull yourself away from the table). If you finish one of the courses early, take the camera over to the children's table and get some comments from the younger folk.

Thanksgiving is one of those occasions when the feel of the video should convey overlapping conversations, the person standing in front of the camera every once in awhile, and blocking the shot, and so on. This is, again, a slice of life, and although the act of videotaping will sometimes interrupt *your* meal, it shouldn't keep people from participating in the holiday as they normally would.

Now it's time for dessert. You've been taping either continuously or in approximately five-minute chunks. People are now satiated and sitting back from the table, children are most likely running around again or are on parents' laps. If you haven't heard these conversations during the meal, you might encourage people to talk about some holiday memories. Ask questions like:

★ Can you remember some particularly fun, poignant, or out-of-the-ordinary celebrations?
★ Is there something about this year's holiday that makes it special?
★ (For the children.) What has been your favorite part of the day, and what will you remember most about this Thanksgiving?

You have a few choices for the end of your video:

★ Around the table, with satisfied guests and the remnants of a memorable meal, have someone voice-over the final tally of the spread: "Seventeen-pound turkey, ten pounds of potatoes, four vegetable dishes, three batches of homemade rolls, two casseroles of sweet potatoes with marshmallows, three bottles of wine, four pumpkin pies—and fourteen happy people."

★ Take the camera off the tripod and shoot highlights of the cleanup (don't use this as an excuse to avoid helping). Go for the busy activity in the kitchen, clearing the table, small children trying to help. . . .

★ Ask for final comments from the oldest and the youngest people at the dinner. Maybe the matriarch or patriarch of the family will share some wonderful thoughts of holidays past and to come. Get some video of the new baby who has just experienced his or her first Thanksgiving. Then arrange for a shot of the oldest and the youngest together.

★ Are there several families at your festivities? Gather them together and have them convey any special Thanksgiving thoughts.

★ Corral the children and ask them what they think Thanksgiving means. Ask them what they liked best about the day—and what they didn't like. Have them tell you what they're thankful for.

★ You might look for a shot or two of guests relaxing after the big meal, a quiet conversation, someone asleep in a chair. Then a quiet voice-over stating this is the end of a great Thanksgiving Day.

16
BAPTISMS,
BAR MITZVAHS,
AND BAT MITZVAHS

THE COMMON THREAD uniting these events is religious ceremony followed by a social event. In the case of bar mitzvahs and bat mitzvahs—the ceremonies that mark respectively a boy's and a girl's arrival at adulthood—the professionally produced video is, for some families, a must. A baptism—the ceremony that affirms one's dedication to his or her faith—can be very short and simple, or a more elaborate, part of a church service, depending on the religious denomination of the family. Whatever you are planning, home video documentation will add immeasurably to the joy of these important family days.

The single most important piece of information you need before taping any part of a religious service in a church or synagogue is . . . permission. Don't show up with your video equipment, then get bent out of shape if a priest, pastor, or rabbi tells you taping is not allowed inside. Do yourself a favor: either meet with or call the appropriate official well before the big day.

If your church or synagogue does not allow taping, you'll be able to get everything but the service. Even though your tape will lack the ritual, you'll still be able to capture the family's emotions and celebration on tape.

If your church or synagogue does allow taping, it will most likely be the same type of taping that it would allow for a wedding—a camera on a tripod that is not to be moved during the ceremony. A tripod is a necessity for the bat or bar mitzvah because the service may be lengthy. A baptism usually lasts only a few minutes and because of the nature of the service—most commonly, an infant's being anointed with water—a hand-held camera may give you a better vantage point.

Whatever the case, visit the church or synagogue before the service and determine the best place to stand or to put your tripod. If your camera position will be a great distance (twenty to thirty feet) from the service, consider renting or borrowing a long-range microphone. You'll then be able to hear what is taking place.

Remember also to check out the light levels. If you think you'll need more light, first get the approval of your clergyperson and give assurances that you will make it as unobtrusive as you can. Even though some churches and synagogues may allow cameras, setting up extra lights may be too much. Make sure that the priest, pastor, or rabbi approves of your location selections to avoid any last-minute snags. Preparation is the watchword for the day, and, as for most things in life, you can never be too prepared.

BAPTISMS

The ritual of baptism may range from a clergyperson in a church simply making a sign of the cross on an infant's forehead to an outdoor ceremony where children and adult baptismal candidates, wearing plain robes, are dipped into a river, lake, or pool. For the purposes of this book, we will address the most likely type of baptism in a young family, that of an infant or small child.

The first thing to do is find a volunteer to videotape the baptism ceremony. If you're the mom or dad, you will be in the ceremony, so you won't be able to tape it too. Find a relative or friend who will be up to that task. It won't be difficult since all we're talking about is a small amount of taping and most of that from a stationary position. However, make sure that your relative or friend knows how to operate your camera. Give the person time to practice with the equipment so she will feel comfortable with the zoom and focus, and so she'll be certain to know when the camera is on "record."

As always, think beginning, middle, end, which in this case will be preparation, ceremony, celebration. Start your tape the morning of the baptism with some shots of the infant either waking or perhaps being fed. A closeup of the baby with the voice-over, "Good morning, little Thomas. It's Sunday, May 19, and it's christening day." Stop tape, then begin recording again when you're dressing the baby. If there is to be a family gathering before the church service, get some highlights on tape—relatives cooing over the infant, children interacting with the baby, dad and mom with the little one.

Note: If the person who will tape the baptism is coming over to your house before church, take time to review the operation of your camcorder. Or ask the person to meet you at church a few minutes early so you can run through everything.

At the church have your camera operator shoot some video of the family entering the main lobby. Out of courtesy to others, this is probably all you can hope for unless your church is very relaxed about camcorders. If that's the case, shoot some of the family entering the church, comments from friends as they see the baby, then stop tape. Once the family is seated, shoot a few seconds of the baby being held, adjusting to the new surroundings, or sleeping peacefully. Your camera operator should be given an aisle seat so that she can quickly and unobtrusively stand up to begin taping.

Most churches give out a bulletin containing the order of worship, which will tell when the baptism will take place. Make sure your camera operator gets a bulletin so she'll be ready to go. At the time of the baptism, the camera operator should stand up with the family and move to the prearranged position. Ideally, she should be able to see family, baby, and clergyperson. However, since baptisms are frequently held at a baptismal font with the participants encircling it, the camera operator might have to shoot the scene from over someone's shoulder. If so, the people closest to the camera should be aware and be asked not to move around much, as they might block the shot. Stop recording once the ceremony is over and the family members return to their seats.

After the church service, your friend can continue to tape, or mom and dad can take over for awhile. Outside the church (if weather

The ideal camera angle will allow you to see all participants clearly.

allows) record remarks from the family, church members greeting the baby, and final words from the clergyperson as everyone is departing.

Pick up the recording once you're at the scene of the celebration, which usually comes in the form of a meal after the church service. It most frequently is at the home of the baby's family but may take place anywhere—at a relative's, a friend's, or a restaurant.

At any rate, throughout this party think highlights. Look for shots of relatives and friends holding the baby, comments from cousins and siblings about the baby, and—if this is a typical infant who doesn't know this day from any other—shots of the baby sleeping, blissfully oblivious of the celebration in his name. Make sure you also have some coverage of the feast and comments from all at the table on the remarkable array of food.

There are several ways to end your tape. You can record the baby sleeping and whisper a voice-over that the christening day has come to an end. Or, mom and dad can take turns videotaping, and share some thoughts on the day. If that friend is still around, ask her to videotape a family portrait of as many family members as you can gather. Still another idea is to end the piece while the baby is being fed; record twenty to forty seconds of the peacefulness of the feeding, with every thing quiet except for the baby's sounds. Following this, voice-over that this is the end of baby's special day.

BAR MITZVAHS AND BAT MITZVAHS

The first thing you should do is go back and read what we wrote about weddings. Bar mitzvahs and bat mitzvahs are major events and the celebration is sometimes on a scale of what a family might do for a wedding. Videotaping the bar mitzvah or bat mitzvah is something that is done almost as a matter of course, but how you produce that vid-eotape can, as at a wedding, mean the difference between a warm family tape and a more distant but professionally produced produc-tion. As we suggest in the chapter on weddings, why not combine both professional video and home video to give you the best of both?

Your camcorder will give you what the pros cannot—behind-the-scenes planning, shopping for special outfits, anticipation of, and per-haps anxiety about, the special day. The story of this video is the story of one member in your family. Remember to spotlight that child, but not in a way that the camcorder becomes an added pressure on them at this rather intense time.

To begin, we realize that thirteen is a very special age—an age when adolescents might not want mom and dad poking and prying too much. But try to open your video with your child practicing the Haftarah, or a selection from the Torah, that he or she will have to sing in Hebrew during the service. You might be opening this video with a shot of a closed door, and muffled singing behind it, or you might be in the room with the child. If you take the closed-door approach, voice-over: "This is Jonathan, practicing for the big day, May the eighteenth." If you're taping the child face to face, you might ask him to introduce the piece—"It's April 16th and I'm practicing for my bar mitzvah. It's a little over a month away, and I'm nervous already."

How is the family planning the celebration? Is the kitchen table filled with invitations? Menu suggestions? Does a contract for a ban-quet-room rental lie on it? Have the child and family members sit around the table and review the plans so far. The child might say, "We've sort of got the menu planned; we will probably go for a Chi-nese selection, since that's my favorite food. We're still undecided about decorations, though. I want neon colors and a DJ for music."

Taking the camcorder along on a shopping trip with an adolescent may prove an exercise in frustration—his frustration with you for doing anything that embarrassing. Suppose you run into someone he knows? Depending on how much your child will let the camcorder participate, shoot at least a couple of try-ons in stores or maybe a modeling for the camera once the final choice has been made. If you're thinking of fabric stores, patterns, and home sewing, take the camera along and get some highlights of looking through the pattern books, discussing the merits of various styles, and walking through the aisles of fabric. Remember, think highlights.

The day of the ceremony will be hectic for the whole family. The anxiety of the religious service coupled with the anticipation of the big family gathering makes for an excited but frantic preparation time. However, designate a family member to record highlights of the child's preparation—perhaps a shot of him dressed in his new outfit, and final comments before leaving for the synagogue about his hopes for the day. If there is time, have the parents give their feelings about what is to take place on this day and the special meaning the bar or bat mitzvah has for them. If you'll be taping the ceremony yourself, double-check your camera equipment; you should be carrying extra batteries and tape.

If you have hired a professional crew to tape the ceremony, certainly use the time before the service to meet with them and review your priorities for the taping. If you're doing it solely on home video, get your tripod and camera set up and run a check of your batteries and tape.

Just before the service begins, have your camera operator (yourself, family member, or friend) move to the preset position. Begin taping as the rabbi and the child enter and take their places on the Bimah (the raised platform where the Torah selections will be given). This will set the scene for the bar or bat mitzvah portion, so don't think that you must get the entire service on tape, unless you want to. That decision depends entirely upon your family. (If you do intend to tape the entire service, make sure those batteries are charged and you have adequate tape.)

Throughout the service think coverage. That is, stay with wide or medium shots most of the time and use your zooms sparingly. You don't want to risk going for an arty closeup shot and miss your child and the rabbi moving to the Holy Ark to get the Torah. However, don't go to the other extreme and stay so wide that you miniaturize the participants. Think head to toe—frame up your shot so that you have a little room above the head of the tallest person, and a little room below that person's feet. That should be wide enough for most of the service.

As your child begins chanting the Haftarah, zoom in more closely so that only the child is in the shot. Be prepared to zoom out as the rabbi announces the first aliyah, or honor. Make sure you're on a wide shot by the end of the rabbi's announcement so that you can see the family member, relative, or friend approaching for the next reading. If there are to be many honors, don't shoot the people returning to their seats. If there are a half dozen participants, you'll merely be going back and forth, back and forth with your camera. Stay on the bar/bat mitzvah child and the rabbi.

As the chanting of the haftarah ends, the bar/bat mitzvah is, technically, over. Unless you're taping the entire service, this will conclude your taping. Be sure you don't stop recording, though, until your child has returned to his position on the Bimah. This would be an appropriate time to slowly zoom in for a closeup of your child's face, hopefully filled with pride and a sense of accomplishment, and relief.

If you intend to tape periodically throughout the service, be ready to begin taping again as the final prayers near. Record the rabbi's ending words while on a wide shot so that you will be able to see the bar/bat mitzvah child's family approaching the Bimah to offer their congratulations. Depending on the emotion of this scene, tape a minute or so. If all you're shooting is a crush of people, stop tape; this will look monotonous after a short time.

As quickly as you can after the ceremony, get to the bar/bat mitzvah child for a comment about the service. This might mean having a family member or friend pack your tripod and other equipment while you with camera make your way through the crowd to your child. Or give the camera to someone (who knows how to operate your camcorder) and let him elicit comments from the child. If you do, take two seconds to let him know what you want him to do: "Get as close to Jonathan as you can and listen to what everyone is saying to him. Make sure you keep him always in the picture." Be certain you give this person a time limit—"Only tape for five minutes." The results will certainly look home video, but that's exactly what you want. You will most likely see mistakes you wouldn't have made, but regard them as all in the spirit of the day.

Before we jump into the party portion of this day, we feel compelled to remind you, again, of our documentation versus participation caution. This is the type of party that you, as a family member, should be right in the middle of. However, because you are a family member, you will also want documentation of the event.

Our advice: select two or three friends or family members who will be willing to take on videotaping duty during the party. You can even make assignments:

Friend/Relative 1: Entrance of family into party, bar/bat mitzvah child's dance with parent, highlights of limbo party game.

Friend/Relative 2: Family toast to child, child's response, quick comments from child and immediate family as meal begins, dancing of the hora.

Friend/Relative 3: Candid comments from relatives and friends as people arrive at the party, candlelighting honors, family portrait near the end of the party.

If your friends follow their assignments, the camera can then be passed from one to another. This way everyone can participate in the celebration. Let the parents serve as the ones to whom the camera always returns. This way they enjoy the party and shoot highlights as they see them.

If you have contracted professionals to tape your party, consider the advice we gave for taping weddings (Chapter 12). Have one or two family members or friends stick to the "hired hands" like glue and direct them to the must have shots—the family matriarch or patriarch, the relatives who traveled a great distance to be there, the candid shots of the bar/bat mitzvah child acting more like a little one than the adult he or she became a short time ago.

Most important, remember, again, that this is a celebration of one child. The child doesn't need to be in every shot but should be the focus of your video. Don't lose the youngster somewhere after his or her arrival at the party. To the best of your ability, have the child in the video with Aunt Sue and Uncle Herman instead of merely talking with them. Go for candid shots of the child's acting silly with friends, talking with older relatives, or just basking in the glory of the day. Remember, think shots of about ten seconds, unless you're recording a conversation or an activity, like the dance with the child's parent, or the hora.

As to the ending, this day will have been exhausting for the entire family. From the high of the party, the conclusion of your tape should return to the pride in the accomplishment of the bar/bat mitzvah child. If only family members remain at the party, you might want to gather them and shoot your ending at the party location. Or you might want to leave the image of the party on tape as fast-moving highlights and conclude your tape with the family back home.

Whatever location you decide, go for a nice family ending to this notable day. Ask parents, siblings, other important people in your child's life what the day meant to them, what the highlight was, and what their hopes for the child are. Save your youngster's replies to your questions for the end. Your questions might run like this:

★ Does he feel any different?
★ Did the day satisfy his expectations?
★ Has the day begun any changes in his life?
★ How does the child feel about himself, his place in the family, and his accomplishment?

Close your video with a medium shot of the bar/bat mitzvah child.

BRIS

The bris is the traditional Jewish ceremony of circumcising a newborn male. Although it may seem slightly off the wall to tape such an event, we have spoken with people who did. Since this is a religious ceremony followed by a celebration, it seems appropriate to discuss the taping here.

The bris usually takes place at the home of the newborn. The ceremony itself is not long and is performed in front of family and friends. The people we spoke to wanted to tape the bris because it was a singular event in the newborn's life. The point was not to get the ceremony itself on tape, but to record the gathering of friends and family to witness the ritual and celebrate the birth of the child.

If you're contemplating taping your child's bris, we'd advise you to follow the schedule we suggested for baptisms. You will want the same type of video. In taping the bris, shoot everything but the ceremony itself. For a nice opening record the baby and family before guests arrive. Then tape highlights as guests arrive, as the rabbi and moel (the one who performs the ritual) arrive, and as the opening prayers begin. After that we'd suggest not taping until the baby is again in the arms of a parent or family member. The people we talked to who had taped the bris felt the day was important to mark, but they had no interest in reliving those rather traumatic couple of minutes in their child's life.

The toasts to the new baby, the comments from guests about the baby, the general feeling of happiness and gaiety in celebrating this new life are the goals of this video. Again, this ritual may not be for everyone, but if you want to shoot it, there's no reason why you can't produce a tape that's enjoyable to watch.

17
FAMILY REUNIONS

LET'S FACE A FACT—family re-
unions are rare. We're not talking about the usual summer picnic get-
togethers most families have. We're talking about full-blown, sixty-
person gatherings with all the cousins and nephews, grandparents and
babies. The family reunion that's lucky to take place once in ten
years—and then only if you're close-knit. Some families don't have
them even that often and some families never have them at all. If an
event like this takes place only once or twice in your lifetime, what
more does it take to be a special occasion begging for video
immortality?

When the big day does arrive, we can guarantee that your camcorder won't be the only one there. The whole family will be out in full
video force and everyone will be looking for the same thing: capturing
the fun and excitement of this very special occasion.

You, however, will be at the head of the video pack. You have
learned a key secret to making great videos and they haven't. That
secret? Look for quality, not quantity.

Our ever-present problem of balancing documenting and participating becomes even more of a problem at family reunions. Since you will want to participate in everything, you may have to force yourself to shoot videos. Come on, be honest with us. What would you rather be doing, eating barbecue and playing softball, or lugging around a camcorder?

So face reality. If you want any of the day on videotape, you will have to sacrifice some of your time. It's only natural that you will sometimes feel as if you are being pulled in two directions, as if shooting videos is somehow diminishing your enjoyment of the day. That's to be expected. But as long as you keep looking for quality moments and shoot as often as you can, both you and your videos will come out winners at the end of the day.

One of the best ways to balance out your day is to enlist someone else to do most of the recording. If you have a willing friend, consider having him come along and shoot a master tape of the entire day. He would be free to roam from group to group and shoot whatever looked interesting, and you would be free to wander about and catch up with distant relatives. Later, a copy of the tape would be made available to whoever wanted it. If you can work something like this out, you will end up with the best of both worlds—the coverage your friend shoots and the personal, family videos you shoot on your own.

Whoever does the videotaping should keep an eye open for those special video moments. To give you an idea of what you should look for, here are some examples of quality moments that will make your videos the best of the show.

CATCH THE PERSONALITIES OF YOUR FAMILY

★ The best way to capture people on tape is to get in close. You can never go wrong shooting tight groups and lots of closeups. May we also suggest that you avoid, except in humor, all group shots of people waving at the camera. Wide, waving shots don't have much personality. Closeups do.

★ Look for groups that are laughing and having a good time. Laughter is infectious and happy people will always look great on video. A good place to start is with the people who are playing games. Another is wherever the children are playing. If they are having a great time, try using them to loosen up other people.

★ Shoot a little video of everyone. Since your video is going to be so stunning, everyone will want a copy of it. And since everyone will see it, they'll love it even more when they see a little bit of themselves.

★ Don't get so carried away that you forget to capture yourself on tape. After all, how great a video will it be if you're not in it?

★ Look for fun shots of the children playing. Cousins who don't see much of each other will quickly overcome their shyness. Videotaping some of their play will help document the bonds that are beginning to grow. These children won't be young for very long so these scenes will be a special part of your tape.

★ Make it a point to talk to your elderly relatives. Sadly, they may not be around much longer, so be sure you record them on tape. A very special quality moment can be created by getting elderly relatives and kids together. Children will always make adults feel younger and adults somehow make kids more talkative. If you have the opportunity to make this match, jump at it. No matter how it comes out, you will still have a special video-bridging of the years.

★ Look for a couple of occasions where you can shoot videos while people are shooting stills. It's always fun to look back and see the "live" video of a moment that's been captured in a still photo.

★ Keep an eye open for sneak-up-on-them videos. Some of the most precious moments are captured when people aren't aware that you are recording them. Maybe grandpa giving wheelbarrow rides to his grandchildren or auntie telling stories to a group of four-year-olds.

VIDEO TIPS TO KEEP IN MIND

★ *Think of video highlights.*

★ *Think of copies.* Shoot a little of everyone, not just your immediate family.

★ *Use lots of identifying voice-overs.* Make sure you have an introduction to your reunion tape. And don't hesitate to do an off-camera voice-over pointing out who's who, especially if people are some distance away.

★ *Think unusual.* Look for shots nobody else is likely to think of. Try setting up your camcorder on a tripod and recording a wide shot during the group family photo. All the jostling and fooling may be great moments to catch (more on this later.)

★ *Don't forget to look for fun.* You and your camcorder can create fun as well as document it. When everyone is loading into their cars at the end of the day, try poking your camcorder through an open car window or walking alongside as the car backs out the driveway.

A FUN FAMILY REUNION VIDEO OUTLINE

Create an opening. If you've got a few extra minutes why not come up with an original opening for your videotape? If there is a horseshoe pit nearby, write "A ——— FAMILY REUNION, AUGUST 1992" in the sand. Shoot five or ten seconds of this title as the opening.

If you are pressed for time, at least shoot a wide panning shot of the area while doing a voice-over stating the occasion, date, and location. Never let yourself feel that an opening shot is silly and not worth the time. The opening shot always sets the tone for the rest of the video to follow.

On with the day. Now to the heart of the day, those shots that will make your video complete. It's important to get close to most of your subjects, so don't hang back. Most of your videos should be shot no more than ten feet from them.

★ Start with some fun and laughter. Two or three children are playing around with the croquet set. Get down to their eye level and shoot thirty to forty seconds (varying your shots, of course) of their banging things with croquet mallets.

★ Are grandma and grandpa watching the action from the comfort of a couple of lawn chairs? Stroll over to them, kneel down to their eye level, and do a mini-interview. Ask them about their day, what they're enjoying the most, and if they'll tell you about the last family reunion.

★ It looks like a heated volleyball game is under way in the side yard. This is a great opportunity to get a lot of your family on tape at one time. Position yourself next to the net and follow the action back and forth awhile. Look for the group interaction that comes from cousins teasing one another and trying to spike the ball down each other's throat.

★ Let's go back to the horseshoe pits again. No picnic is complete without the clanging of steel against steel. The best angle here is behind the pit looking toward the team pitching its shoes. After thirty seconds or so, stop tape, move to the opposite pit, then shoot a bit of the opposing team. If time permits, stay until the game is nearly over. You then can catch the excitement of the victorious team.

★ Is it getting close to food time? If so, wander into the kitchen to cover some of the action there. Be sure you bring that cheerful personality we mentioned and don't hesitate to interact with people while you are shooting. Record shots of the food being prepared and get plenty of tight groups of the people working and talking. Definitely get the famous family recipes on tape, and ask those who brought the dishes why they're family favorites and what are their recipe secrets.

★ Now that you're hungry, check out the food action over by the barbecue grills. Get down close, at burger level, and shoot the chefs through the smoke and flame. Stop tape, stand up and get clear of the smoke, and roll again, getting some closeups of the chefs. Maybe you could offer a voice-over toast to their good work?

★ While the cooking continues look around for some tight group shots of cousins, aunts, and uncles talking and catching up on things. Get close to each group and record thirty seconds or so of each. If you can't get around to everybody, shoot ten-second bits of the more distant groups.

★ Not that shooting videos is more important than eating but try to grab a wide shot of your hungry relatives as they sit down to the much-awaited meal. All you want is a ten-second shot to show everyone enjoying the picnic part of the day.

★ After lunch may be a good time to look for some of those sneak-up-on-them videos. Maybe you can catch Grandma with a couple of grandchildren sitting on her lap or grandpa giving a batting lesson. Some of the sweetest videos come from the tender interaction between young and old, so keep an eye open for any of these tender moments.

★ Late afternoon will probably be "silly time" for the children present. Look for those young cousins to be fooling around once again. Maybe they've put on bathing suits and are running through a lawn sprinkler or playing freeze tag in the front yard. A little more video of kids enjoying themselves would nicely enhance your video.

★ Find the babies. Since big family gatherings are so rare, this reunion's babies will be the next reunion's mischief makers. Get shots of babies being cared for—clothing changes, feedings, settling down for naps. A quiet shot of babies sleeping will make a nice ending for this scene.

★ No family reunion is complete without a group photograph. While everyone is gathering, set your camcorder on a tripod or chair and record the entire thing. The best location is behind and off to one side of the person snapping the photo. Let the camera run for the two or three minutes it takes to get everybody together, posed, and photographed.

★ Goodbye time. Even though you'll be right in the middle of it all, try to record some of the first groups to leave for the long drive home. Get close shots of the hugs, kisses, and tears.

Wrapping it up. We hope you are not one of those who needs to leave early for a long drive home. If you are fortunate enough to be among the last at the picnic, look for a shot that says a great day coming to an end. One possibility may be a small group sitting around, relaxing, having a drink, and offering a video toast to a successful family reunion. Another may be a shot or two of sleeping kids (or adults) sacked out on the couch or in the back seat of a car. Whatever you do, don't forget to shoot a closing piece to your video.

If you still have the energy to be creative, return to the horseshoe pit and write "The End" in the sand. Start your shot tight on the letters and slowly zoom out to show a couple of horseshoes lying against the spike. Hold this shot for ten seconds, stop tape, and call it a day.

T I P

Remember. When you are shooting videos of people, get close and be cheerful. If you get close enough to people to be intimate, you never want to appear intimidating. Be talkative and upbeat and you will notice that those you are shooting will instantly relax and open up.

❖❖❖❖❖❖❖❖❖❖❖❖❖❖❖❖❖❖❖❖❖❖❖❖❖❖❖❖❖❖❖❖❖❖❖❖

EPILOGUE

RE YOU HAVING FUN YET?
If you have made it this far, you're probably bursting with tips, ideas, hints, and video trivia. *Fun* is probably not the word that comes to your mind; *overloaded* may be a better word. One thing is certain, if you manage to incorporate at least some of the ideas we've shared with you, your videos will look livelier, have a better technical appearance—and (don't get too excited) won't make your face red when they're shown publicly.

Remember the point we have stressed about striking a balance between documenting and participating. It's so important to make time for family activities, to play with your children, and to enjoy the holidays your family celebrates. If you get even a little of these precious times on tape, pat yourself on the back. But if you forget the camcorder when you go to the Fourth of July picnic, enjoy the picnic and don't give the camcorder another thought. Life is for living first, videotaping second.

A little planning will go a long way toward making your videos more technically polished and more pleasant to watch. Be it a birthday, vacation, or school play, take time to think about what you want to record before the day of the event.

Always remember beginning, middle, end when you tape any event. If your videos tell a story, you'll soon have a library of tapes that are easier to watch than your old jumbles of bits and pieces of everyday life, holidays, and trips.

May we also say that you no longer have any excuse for making all those silly technical mistakes? Now that you know better, it's not okay to leave the camera running, execute whip pans, or have shots that go for fifteen minutes at a time. Ditto for shooting groups of people in front of bright windows so that your video looks as if you had space aliens over for dinner.

And you won't run out of tape or batteries any more, will you? We've taken that excuse away too.

If you're still not 100 percent confident in your newfound technical skills, go back and read Part I again, then get out a spare tape and practice. You can't expect to record like a pro if your camcorder leaves its case only three or four times a year.

Finally, learn to enjoy your home videos. Don't just tape something, then stash your camcorder in the closet. Make it an everyday part of your family. Instead of watching the same old TV show one night, gather your family around and watch some of your own videos. You'll find that watching home videos encourages family members to talk about the fun experiences they shared, to laugh about the silly antics on screen—and to appreciate the fun-loving family they're part of.

Now we leave it up to you. Go pick up that camcorder, grab the kids, and start making your own fun family videos.